Young People's Pocket Thesaurus

H. Wittels and J. Greisman

WARD LOCK LIMITED · LONDON

© Harriet Wittels and Joan Greisman 1982

First published in Great Britain in 1982
by Ward Lock Limited, 82 Gower Street,
London WC1E 6EQ, a Pentos Company

Previously published as The Young People's
Thesaurus Dictionary

Text filmset in Century Schoolbook
by M.S. Filmsetting Limited, Frome

Printed and bound in Great Britain by
Butler & Tanner Limited, Frome and London

British Library Cataloguing in Publication Data

Wittels, Harriet
 Young people's pocket thesaurus.
 1. English language—Synonyms and antonyms—
Juvenile literature
 I. Title   II. Greisman, Joan
 423′.1   PE1591

 ISBN 0–7063–6183–0

Introduction

In this book you will find hundreds of lists of words. Each word in each list means the same thing or nearly the same thing as the other words in that list. Why bother, you may ask, to gather such words together into lists like these? Simply to help you in two ways. First, to give you all the words which are similar in meaning, so that you can choose the word which seems just right for the thought you wish to convey. Second, to introduce to you words you may not already know. Since you know that all words in each group are synonyms (that's the technical name for words similar in meaning), you can easily guess the meanings of unfamiliar words and thereby greatly expand your vocabulary.

In the pages that follow, you will find thousands of words to help you express yourself clearly, effectively, and imaginatively. Remember, you need not stop at the first list you look up. If you don't find precisely the right word, try one of the other words in the list and look *it* up. That way, you will find the resources of the world's richest language at your fingertips.

How to use
the Young People's Pocket
Thesaurus

Finding entry words

The words that have synonyms and antonyms are called entry words.

---

above   overhead, up, aloft, on, upon   *below*

The word **above**, in heavy black type, is the entry word. All entry words are listed in alphabetical order, just like words in a dictionary.

A book of synonyms and antonyms

In this book you will find synonyms and antonyms for words, *not* the definitions and explanations you can find in a dictionary. Synonyms are words that have the same meaning and can therefore be substituted for one another in a sentence.

---

   expensive   costly, high-priced, dear
      cheap
The bicycle was too expensive for him to
   buy.
The bicycle was too costly for him to buy.
The bicycle was too high-priced for him
   to buy.
The bicycle was too dear for him to buy.

If you cannot find a word, it may be that it simply does not have any synonyms. Its definition will be found in a dictionary.

Antonyms are words that have opposite meanings. Many words listed that have synonyms do not have antonyms.

> **army**   legion, forces, troops, military, militia
> **aroma**   fragrance, odour, perfume, scent

Entry words with groups of synonyms
Sometimes an entry word will have synonyms grouped under different numbers. This means that the entry word has more than one meaning, and each meaning has its synonyms.

> **firm**   1 solid, fixed, secure, unyielding, inflexible, stationary, immovable, rigid; 2 company, business, enterprise

With this type of entry word, you must use judgment and common sense in choosing the appropriate group of synonyms. For example, if you wanted to substitute a synonym in the sentence, 'His mother's **firm** was closed for the holiday,' you would choose the group of synonyms following number 2 for **firm**.

Placement of antonyms
Antonyms will be listed immediately after the synonyms, in italic. You will find antonyms for an entry word that has many groups of synonyms, right after each group, unless one antonym fits all the groups. In that case, the antonym will be listed on a separate line, under all the groups, in italic.

> **due** 1 proper, rightful, fitting, just, fair,
>   square, equitable *unfair*; 2 owed, paid
> **bright** 1 shining, clear, vivid; 2 smart,
>   alert, intelligent; 3 pleasant, cheerful,
>   lively *dull*

Entry words with the same spelling

Sometimes an entry word has two different
pronunciations, as well as different groups of
synonyms. In that case, it will be entered twice,
with numbers in front of the entry word itself.

> **1. minute** instant, moment, twinkling
> **2. minute** small, tiny, miniature, slight,
>   negligible, insignificant

Adapting parts of speech

If an entry word can possibly be considered as a
verb, adjective, adverb, or noun, but is treated
here as a verb, you might need to adapt it for use
as one of the other parts of speech.

> **gag** silence, muzzle, muffle, restrain

In this example, **gag** is treated as a verb, as are
all of its synonyms. If you wanted to substitute
synonyms for the noun **gag**, as in the sentence,
'The robber put a **gag** on his victim's mouth,' you
would adapt the verb **gag** in this way:

> **gag** silencer, muzzle, muffler, restraint

A

abandon desert, forsake, leave, give up
entirely, cease, depart, leave undone, discard,
relinquish, surrender, discontinue, quit,
evacuate, withdraw *keep, fulfill, stay with*

abase bring down, make lower, make humble,
demote, degrade, reduce

abashed ashamed, embarrassed, confused,
bewildered, humiliated, mortified

abate reduce, lessen, put an end to, stop, do
away with, decrease, curtail, moderate
increase

abbreviate shorten, curtail, condense, abridge,
contract, reduce, cut, compress *lengthen,
increase*

abdicate renounce, give up, resign, relinquish,
abandon, quit, surrender, vacate *retain*

abhor hate, dislike, detest, loathe, despise, feel
disgust for *love*

abide 1 accept, obey, endure, tolerate; 2 stay,
reside, dwell

ability power, skill, talent, competence,
capacity, capability, efficiency, aptitude
inability

abject wretched, miserable, deserving
contempt

able skilful, capable, having power, competent,
efficient, qualified *incapable*

abnormal irregular, eccentric, odd, monstrous,
insane, unnatural *normal, sane*

aboard on board, on (or into) a ship, train or
aeroplane

abolish cancel, exterminate, destroy, put an
end to, do away with, wipe out *retain*

abominable hateful, disgusting, very
unpleasant, dreadful, awful, horrible,
atrocious, obnoxious, detestable *pleasant*

abound plentiful, well supplied, filled, teem with, overflow *be scarce*

about 1 concerning, of, upon; 2 nearly, almost, approximately; 3 around; 4 ready to, on the point of

above overhead, up, aloft, on, upon *below*

abreast alongside, side by side, lined up, beside

abroad overseas, away, outside one's country

abrupt sudden, hasty, short, curt, unexpected

absent away, lacking, truant

absolute complete, perfect, thorough, entire, total, essential, positive, supreme *partial*

absolve forgive, cleanse, discharge, pardon, excuse, acquit *blame*

absorb take in, soak up, incorporate, integrate, engross, assimilate, sponge, suck up

abstain refrain, withhold, do without *pursue*

abstract 1 unconcrete, apart from any real thing *concrete*; 2 difficult, hard to understand *clear*; 3 remove, take away, deduct *add*

absurd foolish, ridiculous, not true, unbelievable, impossible, ludicrous *meaningful, sensible*

abundance plenty, large amount, great quantity, profusion *insufficient, not enough*

abuse mistreat, severely scold, injure, damage, ill-use *appreciate*

accelerate hasten, speed up, quicken, hurry *slow down, delay*

accent emphasis, stress on syllables of a word, tone, pronunciation, inflection

accept adopt, believe, approve, take what is offered, consent to *deny, dissent*

accessory addition, extra, contributory, assistant, accomplice, supplement

accident mishap, injury, casualty, chance, event

acclaim applaud, shout welcome, approve
disapprove, reject

accommodate oblige, have room for, supply,
conform

accomplice partner in crime

accomplish do, carry out, finish, complete,
fulfill, perform, achieve, realize *neglect*

accord agreement, conformity, harmony
disagreement

account 1 story, reason, information,
description, tale, statement; 2 list, sum,
record

accumulate collect, store up, increase,
assemble, gather, compile, amass

accurate correct, exactly right, perfect, all
right *wrong*

accuse blame, charge, impeach, indict,
denounce *absolve*

accustom make used to, familiarize, addict,
condition

ache continuous pain, hurt, throb

achieve accomplish, carry out, do, finish,
complete, fulfill, perform, realize *fail*

acknowledge admit, recognize, make known,
answer, accept, grant, concede *dissent*

acquaint make familiar, inform, notify, teach,
tell, enlighten

acquiesce agree, submit, assent, concur,
consent, comply, succumb *dissent*

acquire gain, obtain, get as one's own, secure,
earn *lose*

acquit declare not guilty, absolve, forgive,
cleanse, discharge, pardon, excuse *blame*

acrid sharp, bitter, stinging, nasty, biting,
harsh *sweet, pleasant*

act 1 do, perform, behave; 2 pretend; 3 law

action 1 behaviour, thing done, performance,
way of working; 2 battle

active lively, working, energetic, vivacious, dynamic, animated, spirited *idle, lazy*

activity movement, use of power, energy, thing to do, action

actual real, factual, true, genuine, concrete, authentic *nonexistent*

acute sharp and severe, shrewd, discerning, quick, astute, keen, smart *dull*

adamant firm, unyielding, obstinate *yielding*

adapt make fit, make suitable, modify, change, alter, vary, adjust

add put together, increase, sum up, total, join, unite *subtract*

address 1 apply oneself; 2 speech, greeting; 3 abode, home

adept skilful, expert, apt, proficient *unskilful*

adequate sufficient, enough, satisfactory, ample, plenty *inadequate, insufficient*

adjacent near, adjoining, next to, touching, bordering, neighbouring

adjoin be next to, be close to, be side by side, connect, come in contact with

adjourn postpone, end, put off until a later time, discontinue, suspend, recess, dissolve

adjust arrange, set just right, adapt, make fit, make suitable, modify, change, alter, vary

admirable praiseworthy, excellent, very good, commendable, deserving *unfavourable, objectionable*

admit 1 consent, confess, acknowledge *deny*; 2 allow to enter, induct, receive

admonition warning, advice, reminder, caution, word to the wise, tip

adopt choose, assume, take to oneself, give a home to, accept as one's own *reject*

adore love and respect, worship, idolize, cherish, admire, revere *hate*

adorn beautify, decorate, ornament, garnish, glamorize

adroit smart, clever, adept, skilful, expert, apt, proficient *unskilful*

adult full-grown, grown-up, mature, developed, of age *immature*

advance move forward, promote, progress, proceed *retreat, revert*

advantage benefit, upper hand, leverage, gain *disadvantage*

adventure unusual experience, undertaking, enterprise, event, happening, occurrence, exploit, project, incident

adverse unfriendly, hostile, unfavourable, contrary, opposite, harmful

adversity distress, misfortune, hardship, affliction, grief, disaster, trouble *prosperity*

advertise announce, notify public, call attention to *conceal, hush*

advice counsel, plan, suggestion, recommendation, instruction, direction, tip

advocate 1 recommend publicly, speak in favour of, defend, support; 2 a lawyer *oppose*

affable courteous, pleasant, friendly, sociable, gracious, approachable, amiable, communicative *unsociable, unfriendly*

affair occasion, occurrence, event, happening, matter, concern, business, party, festivity

affect influence, sway, move, persuade

affirm assert, confirm, ratify, state, pronounce, declare, endorse, certify *veto, deny*

afflict cause pain, trouble, bother, distress greatly, disturb, perturb, agitate *soothe*

affluent wealthy, abundant, plentiful, ample, rich, bountiful, well-off, well-to-do, well-fixed *poor*

afford 1 have the means; 2 yield, supply, furnish

affront an open insult, offense, provocation

afraid frightened, fearful, scared, cowardly *courageous*

after 1 later than, following, next, subsequently *before*; 2 behind; 3 in search of, in pursuit; 4 because of; 5 in spite of, despite

again another time, once more, anew, afresh, repeatedly

against in opposition to, versus *with*

age 1 time of life, period in history; 2 grow, old, mature, ripen

aggravate make worse

aggregate total, amount to, add up, accumulate, compile

aggression attack, assault, offence, invasion *defence*

aggressive belligerent, offensive, hostile, militant, combative *peaceful*

aghast astonished, surprised, amazed, astounded, bewildered, thunderstruck, awed, flabbergasted

agile nimble, fast, alert, quick, spry, athletic *dull, slow*

agitate disturb, incite, instigate, excite, stir up, inflame, provoke *calm*

agony suffering, pain, grief, distress, anguish, torture, torment, heartache, woe *peace*

agree consent, assent, accept, approve of, comply *disagree*

agreement pact, contract, understanding, concord, bargain, treaty, alliance, deal *disagreement*

agriculture farming, cultivation, husbandry

ahead in front, before, forward, in advance, leading, winning *behind*

aid help, remedy, relief, assistant, helper, service, benefit *hindrance*

ail 1 trouble, bother, disturb, perturb; 2 be ill, suffer, feel awful, feel sick

aim 1 direct, point, intend, try; 2 purpose,
intention, objective, goal, end, target

airy light, breezy, fanciful, lighthearted, gay,
graceful, merry *grave, gloomy*

aisle passageway, corridor, alley, lane,
channel, artery, opening

alarm 1 startle, arouse, frighten, shock, jar,
jolt, agitate, disturb, unnerve *calm*;
2 signal, call, warning, summons

alcoholic drunkard, inebriate, sot, tippler

alert watchful, wide awake, clear-witted,
attentive, ready, prompt, lively, nimble, on
the job, on one's toes *dull*

alien 1 foreign, different, strange; 2 foreigner

allay lessen, check, quiet, relieve, calm, ease,
pacify, moderate, restrain, alleviate *excite*

allege declare, state

allegiance loyalty, faithfulness, devotion,
fidelity

alley narrow back-street, path, aisle,
passageway, corridor, lane, opening

alliance agreement, pact, contract,
understanding, bargain, treaty

allot distribute, share, divide, assign,
apportion, allocate, budget

allow 1 let, permit, consent, grant, admit;
2 acknowledge, concede, recognize *deny*

allowance allotment, portion, fee, grant,
ration, budget

allure fascinate, attract, charm, tempt,
captivate, infatuate

almighty powerful, great, divine, omnipotent

almost nearly, close to, just about

alms charity, dole, contribution, donation

alone isolated, solitary, solo, lonely,
unaccompanied *accompanied*

aloof away, apart, distant, remote, unsociable,
reserved, standoffish, cool *friendly*

also   too, in addition, as well, besides

alter   make different, change, vary, deviate, modify, diversify   *maintain*

alternate   take turns, switch, interchange

alternative   choice, substitute, replacement

altogether   completely, wholly, entirely, thoroughly, totally   *partly*

always   forever, all the time   *never*

amass   accumulate, collect, heap up, store up, increase, assemble, gather, compile

amaze   surprise, astonish, astound, aghast, bewilder, thunderstruck, flabbergast

ambitious   aspiring, set on, intent upon   *indifferent*

ambush   1 surprise attack, lying in wait; 2 hiding place, trap

amend   change, correct, improve, mend

among   amid, between, surrounded by, in with

amount   sum, quantity, value, measure, price

ample   large, abundant, enough, full, sufficient, plenty   *insufficient*

amuse   entertain, divert, delight, tickle, titillate

anchor   1 fasten, secure, fix, attach; 2 ship hook

ancient   old, aged, antique, archaic, elderly   *young, new*

anecdote   story, tale, yarn, account, narrative, joke

angelic   heavenly, pure, good, lovely, innocent, virtuous, saintly, godly   *devilish*

anger   wrath, ire, rage, fury, annoyance, irritation

anguish   agony, suffering, pain, grief, distress, torture, torment, heartache, woe   *peace*

animated   lively, gay, vigorous, spry, active, vivacious, snappy   *inactive*

animosity   hatred, dislike, ill will, bitterness   *love, good will*

annex 1 add, attach, join, unite with;
   2 something joined, addition, wing, extension

annihilate demolish, destroy, abolish, end,
   wreck

announce make known, proclaim, report,
   broadcast, declare, state, notify, tell

annoy tease, vex, disturb, irritate, make
   angry *please, calm*

answer reply, respond

antagonize oppose, cross, go against, counter,
   provoke, embitter *soothe*

anticipate expect, await, hope for, foresee

antics capers, pranks, funny gestures, practical
   jokes, tricks

antipathy hatred, strong dislike *love*

antique ancient, old, aged, archaic *new*

anxious 1 uneasy, concerned, fearful, troubled,
   bothered, perturbed, agitated, worried
   relaxed; 2 eager, desirous, keen

apathy indifference, unconcern, lethargy
   feeling, interest

aperture opening, hole, gap

apologize beg pardon, ask forgiveness, express
   regret, offer an excuse

appal horrify, shock, dismay, terrify, stun

apparatus equipment, gear, rig, tackle,
   furnishings

apparent plain, seeming, obvious, evident,
   clear *hidden, mysterious*

apparition ghost, illusion, vision, phantom,
   dream, fantasy

appeal ask earnestly, beg, plead, implore,
   entreat

appear seem, look

appease calm, satisfy, quiet, allay, lessen,
   check, relieve, ease, pacify, moderate,
   restrain, alleviate *irritate*

appetite hunger, desire, craving

applaud approve, praise, cheer, hail, acclaim, clap *disapprove, reject*

appliance tool, machine, device, instrument, implement, utensil

apply 1 request, ask, petition; 2 put on, administer

appoint elect, choose, name, vote for, assign, nominate

appreciate 1 value, enjoy, think highly of, respect, admire, be grateful *dislike*; 2 grow, rise in value

apprehend 1 fear, dread; 2 seize, arrest, capture, take prisoner *release*

apprehensive afraid, worried, anxious, uneasy, concerned, fearful, troubled, bothered, agitated, perturbed *relaxed*

apprentice beginner, learner, novice, amateur

approach 1 come near, advance *retreat*; 2 entrance, inlet, passageway, access

appropriate 1 suitable, proper, fitting, becoming *inappropriate*; 2 take possession of, take for oneself, take for some special purpose *misappropriate*

approve like, think well of, accept, ratify, endorse *disapprove, frown on*

approximate 1 approach, near, close; 2 rough *exact*

apt 1 likely, suitable, appropriate, proper fitting *unlikely*; 2 quick to learn, bright, clever, acute, sharp, shrewd, discerning, astute, keen, smart

aqueduct waterway, gully, canal, channel, pipe

arbitrary unreasonable, wilful *fair, reasonable*

arbitrate settle, referee, umpire, negotiate, mediate

ardent enthusiastic, eager, zealous, earnest, sincere, fervent, passionate, warm *apathetic, cool*

arduous difficult, strenuous, hard, laborious *easy*

area 1 extent, space, region, expanse, zone, territory, district, section, neighbourhood; 2 size

argue reason, object, persuade, bicker

arid 1 dry, waterless *wet, fertile*; 2 dull, stuffy, flat, unimaginative *colourful*

arm 1 part of a body; 2 weapon; 3 equip, defend, fortify, empower

armistice peace, truce, treaty, agreement, pact, contract, understanding, concord, alliance, deal

army legion, forces, troops, military, militia

aroma fragrance, odour, perfume, scent

arouse stir, excite, awaken, move, provoke, pique, kindle, inflame, foment, stimulate, agitate, disturb, shake

arrange settle, put in order, adapt, fit, classify, catalogue, organize, systematize *confuse, muddle*

arrest stop, check, seize, catch, apprehend, capture, take prisoner *release*

arrive come, reach, get to *depart*

arrogant too proud, haughty, insolent, cavalier *humble, modest*

art 1 drawing, painting, sculpture, design, work, composition, masterpiece; 2 skill, knack, craft, technique

artery 1 blood vessel; 2 main road, aqueduct, channel, pipe

artful 1 crafty, sly, deceitful; 2 skilful, clever, cunning, shrewd, knowing *artless*

article 1 composition, story, essay, report, treatise; 2 object, thing

artificial false, pretended, substitute, ungenuine, unreal, fake, synthetic, imitation, counterfeit *real, authentic*

artless 1 natural, simple, without trickery; 2 without art, unskilled, ignorant *artful*

ascend go up, rise, climb, mount *descend*

ascertain find out, learn, solve, answer, clear up

ashamed embarrassed, humiliated, abashed, mortified *proud*

ask question, find out, inquire, request, invite *answer*

aspect view, look, appearance

aspire seek, desire, be ambitious, aim, strive

assassinate kill, murder, purge

assault attack, offence, onslaught, charge

assemble meet, gather together, congregate, collect, crowd, throng, cluster, group *scatter, disperse*

assent agree, consent, accept, approve of, comply *dissent*

assert declare, state, insist on, affirm, pronounce

asset valuable things, property, funds, wealth, accounts, resources, goods, capital

assign appoint, elect, allot, choose, name, distribute, apportion, allocate

assimilate absorb, digest, soak up, blot up

assist help, aid, support, lend a hand

associate 1 join, connect, combine, unite *dissociate*; 2 companion, partner, ally

assorted various, different, mixed, several

assauge quiet, calm, allay, lessen, check, ease, relieve, pacify, moderate, restrain, alleviate *excite*

assume 1 suppose, take for granted, presume, suspect, understand, believe, think; 2 put on, adopt

assure convince, make certain, promise, guarantee, pledge

astonish surprise, astound, amaze

astound amaze, surprise, astonish

asunder apart, separate, divided *together*

asylum refuge, shelter, institution, home, mental hospital

athletic active, strong, muscular, brawny, able-bodied, well-built, sporting, gymnastic

atrocious wicked, cruel, savage, brutal, ruthless, terrible, horrible, dreadful, awful, vile, wretched, contemptible *kind, good*

attach fasten, join, connect, affix, add, put together, increase, unite *detach*

attack raid, siege, bombardment, assault, offence, onslaught, charge, drive, push

attain 1 reach, arrive, come, get to; 2 gain, accomplish, finish, complete, fulfil, achieve, realize

attempt try, endeavour, make an effort

attend 1 be present, visit, go to *be absent*; 2 serve, help, work for, administer to, care for

attention care, courtesy, consideration, concern, thoughtfulness, politeness

attitude viewpoint, standpoint, position, opinion

attract pull, interest, draw, fascinate, allure, charm, tempt, captivate, infatuate *repel*

attractive pleasing, winning, charming, desirable, beautiful *unattractive*

attribute 1 assign, ascribe, give, place, apply; 2 characteristic, quality, trait, nature, feature

audacious bold, daring, foolhardy, arrogant, haughty, insolent, cavalier *shy, humble*

audible hearable, distinct, clear, plain *inaudible*

augment increase, enlarge, expand, raise, extend, broaden, magnify *decrease*

auspicious favourable, fortunate, lucky, promising, timely *unfortunate, untimely*

austere harsh, stern, strict, severe *soft, lenient*

authentic real, reliable, genuine, legitimate, actual, factual, true

authoritative commanding, powerful, influential, official

authorize give power to, legalize, enable, assign

autocrat ruler, monarch, dictator, tyrant

automatic self-acting, spontaneous, self-working *manual*

auxiliary helping, assisting, aiding

avail use, help, benefit, profit, advantage, value, worth, serve

available handy, convenient, ready, at hand, obtainable *unavailable, unobtainable*

avarice greed, lust, desire for money

average 1 usual, ordinary, passable, fair *unusual, extraordinary*; 2 middle, medium *extreme*

averse opposed, unwilling, against, forced, involuntary *willing*

aversion strong dislike, hatred, loathing *love*

avert prevent, avoid, turn away, prohibit *invite*

avid eager, greedy

avoid keep away from, shun, evade, snub *seek*

aware knowing, realizing, conscious, cognizant *ignorant, unaware*

awe fear and wonder, astonishment, surprise, dread, respect, alarm

awful unpleasant, atrocious, wicked, cruel, savage, brutal, ruthless, terrible, horrible, dreadful, vile, wretched *pleasant*

awkward clumsy, ungraceful, cumbersome, ungainly *graceful*

awry wrong, askew, crooked, disorderly,
   twisted *right, straight*

B

background experience, knowledge, training,
   practice
bad evil, wrong, unfavourable *good*
badger 1 question, tease, annoy, torment,
   bother, pester, harass, bait; 2 animal
baffle puzzle, perplex, confound, mystify,
   bewilder
bait 1 badger, question, tease, annoy, torment,
   bother, pester, harass; 2 trap, lure, tempt
balance 1 equalize, weigh, measure, stabilize,
   steady; 2 scale
bald hairless, bare, simple, open, nude,
   uncovered *hairy, covered*
balk be unwilling, jib, shirk, shy, thwart *be
   willing*
ballot vote, choice, poll
balmy mild, soft, gentle, fragrant
ban prohibit, forbid, outlaw, bar, block,
   obstruct, exclude, shut out *allow*
banish exile, expel, force away, drive away,
   deport, outlaw
bank 1 shore, barrier, slope; 2 treasury,
   storage; 3 a row of oars
bar 1 block, obstruct, exclude, shut out, forbid,
   ban, prohibit *allow*; 2 pole, rod, stick;
   3 lawyers as a group; 4 saloon, tavern,
   counter; 5 measured period of time in music
barbarian uncivilized, cruel, coarse, savage,
   uncouth, brutal, uncultured, primitive
   civilized
bare naked, nude, bald, open, uncovered
   covered
barely scarcely, hardly, just

bargain 1 agree, contract; 2 something bought cheaply

barren unproductive, childless, infertile, sterile, blank *fertile, productive*

barrier barricade, obstruction, fortification

barter trade, deal, exchange, swap

base 1 found, establish, set, settle, fix; 2 low, mean, selfish, cowardly, inferior; 3 bottom, foundation, groundwork; 4 station, headquarters

bashful awkward, uneasy, shy, timid, coy *aggressive*

basic essential, fundamental, underlying

batter 1 beat, pound, smash, thrash; 2 mixture

battle struggle, fight, combat, war, contest, conflict *peace*

bawl shout, cry, wail, weep, sob, howl

beach shore, coast, waterfront, seaside

beacon watchtower, signal, alarm, flare

beam 1 shine, smile, glow; 2 timber, bar, shaft

bear 1 carry, endure, withstand, hold, support, produce, yield; 2 animal

bearing 1 manner, air; 2 reference, relation, connection; 3 direction, way, course

beat 1 strike, blow, bat, hit, knock, crack, clout; 2 mix, stir; 3 accent in music; 4 outdo, surpass, win, defeat, triumph

beautiful pretty, handsome, attractive, lovely *ugly*

beckon gesture, motion, invite, signal

before earlier, prior, previously, formerly, in advance *after*

beg ask, beseech, appeal, plead, implore, entreat

begin start, commence, take off *end, finish*

beguile 1 deceive, cheat, trick, dupe, bamboozle; 2 amuse, entertain, charm

behaviour conduct, action, acts, manner
behind 1 after, later than; 2 retarded,
  backward *ahead*
behold see, look, notice, view, perceive,
  observe, sight
believe trust, suppose, think, surmise *doubt*
belligerent warlike, aggressive, offensive,
  hostile, militant, combative *peaceful*
below under, lower, less *above*
bend 1 curve, turn; 2 bow, stoop, kneel;
  3 yield, submit
beneath below, under *above*
benediction blessing, thanks, prayer
beneficial favourable, helpful, profitable,
  useful, advantageous *harmful*
benevolence kindness, generosity, good will,
  charity *ill will*
beseech beg, ask, appeal, plead, implore,
  entreat
beset attack, surround
besides moreover, also, too, in addition, as well
besiege attack, assault, raid, siege, bombard,
  charge
best prime, choice, select
bestial beastly, brutal, cruel, savage
bestow give, put, place, present, award
bet wager, gamble
betray mislead, deceive, trick
better superior, preferable, improved *worse*
between betwixt, among
beware be careful, guard against, take care,
  look out, watch out, look sharp
bewilder confuse, baffle, puzzle, perplex,
  confound, mystify *clarify*
beyond farther, past, exceeding
bias 1 slanting, oblique, diagonal; 2 prejudice,
  prejudgment, sway
bid command, order, direct, instruct, ask,
  invite, enjoin

big   large, important, great, grand, considerable, grown-up, adult, mature   *little, small*

birth   beginning, origin, inception, infancy   *end, death*

bit   1 small amount, piece;   2 harness, restraint

bite   cut with teeth, nip, pierce

biting   sharp, cutting, sneering, sarcastic, acid

bitter   distasteful, unpleasant   *pleasant*

blame   accuse, charge, impeach, indict, denounce, tattle   *absolve*

blank   empty, void, vacant

blast   explosion, blowout, burst, discharge

blaze   1 fire, flame, flare;   2 notch, marking

bleak   bare, chilly, cold, dreary, dismal   *cheerful*

blemish   stain, scar, injury, defect

blend   mix, combine, beat, join, stir   *separate*

blight   1 spoil, ruin, destroy, decay, wither;   2 decaying, disease

blind   1 sightless, visionless;   2 without thought, without judgment

bliss   happiness, joy, delight, glee, elation   *sadness*

bloat   swell, puff up, inflate   *deflate*

block   1 clog, obstruct, hinder   *clear*;   2 lump, solid, mass

blockade   obstruction, barrier, barricade, fortification

bloodthirsty   cruel, murderous

bloom   flourish, thrive, flower, glow, blossom

blossom   develop, flower, bloom

blow   1 puff, breeze;   2 knock, stroke, whack, rap

blowout   burst, explosion, blast

bluff   1 deceive, trick, delude;   2 steep cliff, bank

blunder   stumble, mistake, flounder

blunt 1 dull, unsharp *sharp*; 2 outspoken, candid, frank, straightforward, direct

blur dim, smear, cloud

board 1 mount, embark, get on; 2 committee, cabinet; 3 wood, lumber; 4 food, meals

boast brag, pat oneself on the back

body 1 substance, firmness; 2 the main part, mass, bulk; 3 group, collection, throng, crowd

boil 1 fume, seethe, rage; 2 cook, bubble; 3 swelling, pimple

boisterous violent, rough, noisy, rowdy, tumultuous *serene*

bold 1 defiant, impudent, brazen, arrogant, haughty, insolent, cavalier *modest*; 2 vigorous, free, clear

bolt 1 flee, break away, take flight; 2 lock, fastener

bombard attack, fire upon, shell, torpedo, open fire

bonus extra, more, premium

boom 1 progress, increase, advance, gain, grow, swell, thrive, flourish; 2 thunder, roar, rumble; 3 pole, beam

booty plunder, prize, loot, stolen goods

bore 1 drill, pierce, puncture; 2 make weary, irk

born brought forth, hatched, produced

bother worry, fuss, trouble, concern, annoy

bottom base, foundation, lowest part *top*

bound 1 enclosed, surround; 2 spring back, leap, jump; 3 going, on the way; 4 boundary, limit

boundary bound, limit, border, division, barrier

bountiful fertile, bounteous, generous, plentiful, abundant *scarce*

bout 1 test, contest, trial, struggle, battle; 2 spell, length of time, turn, round

boycott strike, revolt, picket, blackball, ban

bracket 1 couple, join, relate, enclose;
2 support, brace

brag boast, pat oneself on the back

brake stop, slow down, decelerate, curb
accelerate

branch 1 spread, divide, expand; 2 part of a
tree

brand 1 mark, burn, label, tag; 2 kind, sort,
type, stamp

brave courageous, bold, valiant, gallant,
heroic *cowardly*

brawl quarrel, riot, racket, fracas

brawn muscle, strength *weakness*

brazen shameless, immodest, bold, forward
modest

breach break, gap, falling-out, quarrel

break 1 fracture, rupture, crack, burst *heal,
mend*; 2 violation; 3 interruption, interval,
pause, rest, letup

breed raise, produce, train, race, develop, bring
up, cultivate

brevity shortness, conciseness, briefness
length

bribe buy off

bridle 1 restrain, control, check, hold back;
2 harness

brief short, concise, terse, curt *long*

bright 1 shining, clear, vivid; 2 smart, alert,
intelligent; 3 pleasant, cheerful, lively *dull*

brilliant 1 sparkling, bright, shining, clear,
vivid; 2 smart, alert, intelligent *dull, drab*

brisk 1 breezy; 2 spirited, lively, jolly, spry,
energetic, active, quick *dull*

brittle fragile, crisp, breakable, frail *strong,
sturdy*

broad wide, large, expansive, roomy *narrow*

broadcast publish, distribute, scatter,
announce, circulate

broken burst, ruptured, shattered *repaired*
brood 1 ponder, contemplate, study, reflect, consider, meditate; 2 family group
brotherhood bond kinship, relationship, fraternity, fellowship
browse 1 read, scan; 2 feed, graze
bruise injure, hurt, wound *heal*
brusque abrupt, blunt, gruff, curt, harsh, surly *courteous*
brutal coarse, barbarian, cruel, savage *kind*
buckle 1 fasten, clasp, hook, clip; 2 bend, distort, wrinkle; 3 belt, strap, catch, clip
bud sprout, flourish, develop
budget ration, allowance, schedule
buff polish, rub, shine, wax, burnish
build construct, make, create
building construction, structure, establishment, edifice
bulk lump, mass, majority
bulletin message, circular, news, statement, flash, newsletter
bully tease, pester, annoy, badger, torment, bother, harass
bunch group, set, batch, cluster
bundle parcel, package, bale, packet
bungle botch, tumble, blunder
buoyant 1 light, floating, elastic, springy *heavy*; 2 cheerful, lighthearted, carefree *gloomy, sad*
burden load, charge, task, hard work
burglar robber, thief, housebreaker
burly strong, sturdy, brawny *weak*
burn blaze, fire, flame, flare
burnish buff, polish, rub, shine
burrow 1 dig, tunnel, excavate; 2 search, hunt, seek
burst broken, ruptured, exploded
bury cover, conceal, hide, immerse, cache *uncover*

business work, occupation, profession, trade, affair, job

bustle fuss, noise, activity, flurry, ado, action, stir, trouble, commotion, excitement, hubbub, to-do *calm*

busy working, active, occupied, engaged, on the job *idle, inactive*

busybody meddler, gossip, tattletale

buy purchase, pay money for *sell*

by near, beside, at

C

cabin house, cottage, bungalow, hut

cable 1 telegraph, wire; 2 rope, cord, wire

cackle shrill laugh, babble, chatter, prattle

calamity 1 misfortune, mishap, accident; 2 disaster, catastrophe, tragedy

calculate 1 count, compute, figure, estimate, reckon; 2 plan, reason, think, suppose

call 1 cry, shout, yell; 2 speak, ask, command, invite, telephone

calling profession, occupation, trade, vocation

callous hard, unfeeling, insensitive, heartless, cold *sensitive*

calm quiet, still, peaceful, serene, tranquil *excited*

camouflage disguise, masquerade

campaign crusade, drive, cause, movement

canal waterway, aqueduct, gully, duct, tube

cancel wipe out, erase, obliterate, repeal

candid sincere, blunt, outspoken, frank, straightforward, direct

candidate applicant, seeker, nominee

candour frankness, sincerity, fairness

canny 1 shrewd, artful, crafty, skilful, clever, cunning *artless*; 2 cautious, prudent, careful

canopy   cover, awning, shelter, screen
capability   ability, power, fitness, capacity, skill, talent, competency, efficiency   *inability*
capacity   1 size, volume, content; 2 intelligence, mentality, power, fitness; 3 position, function, duty, role
capital   1 important, leading, top, chief; 2 money, funds, stock;   3 city, government seat;   4 large letter
caprice   whim, fancy, fad, unreasonable desire
capsize   upset, overturn, overthrow, tip over
caption   title, heading, headline
captivate   charm, fascinate, delight, bewitch
capture   arrest, seize, imprison, apprehend   *free*
car   automobile, vehicle
caravan   1 group, procession, parade; 2 wagon, van
care   1 thought, worry, attention, concern; 2 protection, charge, supervision, keeping, custody   *neglect*
career   profession, occupation, vocation, calling, trade
carefree   happy, gay, lighthearted, breezy, lively, jolly, spry, energetic, spirited, active   *worried*
careful   cautious, watchful, prudent
careless   reckless, slovenly, sloppy   *careful*
cargo   load, freight, shipment
carnival   fair, festival, fête, jamboree
carp   1 complain, find fault, pick, tear to pieces   *praise*;   2 fresh-water fish
carriage   1 vehicle, conveyance;   2 posture, position, bearing
carry   hold, transport, take
carve   cut, slice
case   1 condition, state, circumstance; 2 covering, box, receptacle;   3 lawsuit, legal action

cast   1 throw, fling, pitch, toss;   2 mould, form, shape;   3 company, troupe, actors

castle   palace, mansion, chateau

casual   accidental, chance, informal, unexpected, natural   *planned*

casualty   misfortune, accident, mishap, injury, fluke

catalogue   1 list, classify, record, group, sort;   2 file

catastrophe   calamity, misfortune, tragedy, disaster, accident

catch   1 take, arrest, seize, apprehend, capture;   2 surprise, discover

cause   motive, reason, interest, basis, grounds

caution   warn, advise, alert, admonish, remind, tip

cavalcade   procession, column, parade

cavalier   1 haughty, contemptuous, arrogant, insolent;   2 gentleman, horseman, knight, escort

cave   cavern, shelter, den, lair

cavity   hole, pit, crater

cease   stop, end, halt, quit, discontinue   *continue*

cede   give up, surrender, yield, relinquish   *acquire*

celebrate   1 proclaim, observe, commemorate;   2 make merry, revel

celebrity   notable, well-known person, somebody   *unknown*

cement   fasten, solidify, secure, weld

censure   blame, reproach, denounce, criticize, condemn   *approve*

centre   middle, heart, core, nucleus

central   main, chief, principal, leading

ceremonious   1 formal, ritualistic, stately, pompous   *informal*;   2 courteous, polite, gracious

certain 1 sure, positive, definite *uncertain*;
2 some, particular, special

certify guarantee, testify, vouch, affirm,
confirm

cessation end, discontinuation, close
continuation

chafe 1 rub, heat, warm; 2 anger, annoy, vex,
disturb, irritate

chagrin embarrassment, mortification,
humiliation, disappointment

chain bind, restrain, fasten, shackle

chairman speaker, presiding officer

challenge confront, question, defy, dare,
dispute, doubt

champion 1 winner, victor, best, choice, select,
conqueror *loser*; 2 defender, upholder,
protector, advocate

chance 1 opportunity, occasion, opening;
2 possibility, probability, likelihood,
prospect; 3 fate, luck, lot

change 1 alter, vary, deviate, substitute,
replace; 2 cash, money, coins

channel 1 waterway, strait, passageway,
corridor, artery; 2 TV station

chaos confusion, disorder, muddle, mix-up
order

chapter section, part, division

character 1 nature, makeup, constitution,
temperament, disposition; 2 actor,
performer, player; 3 letter, sign, symbol;
4 eccentric

characterize describe, distinguish, represent,
portray, picture, depict

charge 1 load, fill, stuff; 2 order, command,
direct, bid; 3 blame, accuse, complain,
denounce, impeach, indict; 4 rate, ask as a
price; 5 attack, rush at

charitable generous, kindly, giving, bighearted *selfish*

charming pleasing, delightful, fascinating, appealing, enchanting, alluring *obnoxious*

charter 1 hire, lease, rent; 2 treaty, alliance

chase 1 follow, pursue, run after; 2 drive away, repulse, reject

chaste pure, clean, virtuous, modest, decent *impure*

chastise punish, beat

cheap 1 inexpensive, low-priced *dear*; 2 common, plentiful, abundant *scarce*

cheat defraud, swindle, beguile, deceive, trick, dupe, bamboozle

check 1 stop, control, restrain, curb, pause, rebuff; 2 prove, mark, verify

cheer 1 comfort, praise, gladden; 2 hope, good spirits, gladness, happiness *sadness*

cherish adore, worship, hold dear, protect, treasure

chide reproach, blame, scold, reprimand, lecture

chief leader, head, authority

chiefly mainly, mostly, above all, especially

child youngster, baby, tot, juvenile, youth, young boy or girl, offspring

chilly cold, cool, brisk, nippy, wintry, snappy *warm*

chisel 1 make, sculpture, carve; 2 engrave, inscribe; 3 tool

chivalrous courteous, gallant, knightly, polite, noble

choice 1 selection, pick, decision, option, alternative, preference; 2 best, cream

choke smother, suffocate, strangle, muffle

chop cut, cleave, sever

chorus 1 choir, group, unison; 2 verse, stanza, refrain

chronic constant, established, fixed, set, lasting, continuing

chronicle   history, story, account, journal, narrative

chum   friend, mate, pal, companion, partner, comrade

circulate   go around, publish, broadcast, distribute, scatter, announce

circumstance   condition, situation, state

citation   1 honourable mention, decoration, medal;   2 summons, subpoena;   3 quotation

citizen   inhabitant, occupant, resident

city   metropolis, municipality, large town

civil   1 public, common, social;   2 ceremonious, courteous, polite   *uncivil*

claim   1 demand, require;   2 right, due, interest, title

clamour   cry out, demand, complain

clamp   fasten, clasp, brace

clarify   explain, refine, make clear, simplify   *confuse*

clash   1 contradict, oppose, disagree, differ, conflict   *agree*;   2 collide, bump, bang, hit

clasp   grasp, buckle, fasten, hook, clip

class   1 rank, grade, quality;   2 group, category, division

classify   organize, group, categorize, sort

clatter   noise, rattle, racket, din

clean   cleanse, purify, wash, tidy   *dirty*

clear   1 remove, eliminate, get rid of   *retain*;   2 free, acquit   *convict*;   3 clean, cleanse, purify, wash, tidy

clemency   mercy, pity, sympathy, compassion, lenience, mildness   *harshness, severity*

clever   skilful, cunning, bright, smart, alert, intelligent   *dull*

client   customer, prospect, patron

climate   weather, elements, atmospheric conditions

climax   1 result, end, conclusion;   2 turning point

climb mount, ascend, rise

clinch 1 seize, grip, cinch, bind, hold, wrap, tie, fasten; 2 establish, ensure, make certain

cling hold, grasp, adhere, stick

cloak 1 hide, conceal, cover, protect; 2 robe, wrap, coat

clog 1 stuff, block, obstruct, choke.; 2 wooden shoe

1. close 1 shut, fasten, lock *open*; 2 end, finish, stop, conclude, terminate *start*

2. close 1 near, approaching, imminent *far*; 2 stuffy, airless, stifling, suffocating

cloudy dark, unclear, overcast, gloomy, dismal

clout rap, bat, hit, knock, strike

club 1 hit, beat, strike, blow, bat, knock; 2 bat, stick; 3 group, society, clique

clue hint, evidence, proof, sign, key, lead

clumsy awkward, ungraceful, ungainly, cumbersome

clutch cling, hold, grasp, adhere, stick

clutter 1 rubbish, trash, debris; 2 confusion, disorder, jumble

coach 1 train, teach, tutor; 2 carriage

coagulate thicken, clot, set

coarse 1 rough, bumpy *fine, smooth*; 2 common, poor, inferior; 3 crude, vulgar *refined*

coast 1 slide, glide, ride; 2 seashore, seaside, waterfront, beach

coax persuade, influence, urge, pressure, push, wheedle

coddle pamper, cater to, spoil, oblige, indulge

code laws, rules, arrangement, system, signal

coerce compel, force

coin 1 invent, make up, devise, originate; 2 money, silver

collapse break down, fail, crash, topple

colleague associate, buddy, friend, companion, partner, comrade

collect   assemble, gather, accumulate, store up
collide   conflict, bump, clash, bang
colony   settlement, community
colourful   vivid, picturesque, bright, gay, rich
  colourless
colourless   dull, uninteresting, flat, dreary
  colourful
colossal   huge, gigantic, vast, enormous,
  immense, mammoth   *insignificant*
column   1 division, section, part;   2 tower,
  pillar, cylinder, monument
combat   battle, struggle, fight, contest,
  conflict, war
combine   join, unite, mix, connect, couple,
  blend, fuse   *separate*
combustible   flammable, burnable, fiery
comfort   console, ease, assure, relieve, cheer,
  gladden
command   1 bid, order, direct, instruct,
  enjoin;   2 power, control
commemorate   honour, celebrate, observe,
  proclaim
commence   begin, start, take off, fire away
commend   1 praise, compliment, approve
  criticize, disapprove;   2 commit, assign, trust
comment   remark, note, observe, mention
commerce   trade, business, dealings
commit   1 entrust, promise, pledge;   2 perform,
  do
committee   council, group, delegation
commodious   roomy, spacious, comfortable
  confined
commodity   product, ware, article
common   1 public, general *private*;   2 usual,
  familiar, ordinary, everyday   *odd*;   3 low,
  crude, coarse, vulgar, poor, inferior   *refined*
commotion   disturbance, tumult, confusion,
  rumpus, ado, action, stir, fuss, trouble,

excitement, row, stir, hubbub, to-do *order, calm*

communicable contagious, catching, transferable, infectious

communicate inform, tell, enlighten, report, convey

community 1 society, people, colony, district, town; 2 ownership together

commute 1 exchange, substitute, replace, switch; 2 travel, move

compact 1 concise, short, brief *lengthy*; 2 agreement, contract, pact, understanding, concord, bargain, treaty, alliance, deal

companion partner, accompanist, friend, pal, comrade, chum

company 1 group, association; 2 business, firm, enterprise; 3 guest, visitors, companions

compare match, liken, measure

compassion clemency, mercy, pity, sympathy, leniency, mildness *harshness, severity*

compatible agreeing, harmonious *incompatible, differing*

compel force, make, require

compensate pay, reward, atone for, balance, make up for

compete rival, vie with

competent able, effective, adequate, capable, qualified, fit *incompetent*

compile gather, collect, assemble, accumulate, store up

complacent self-satisfied, contented *dissatisfied*

complain grumble, squawk, find fault, fret

complement supply, complete, supplement

complete 1 finish, conclude, terminate, end, clean up, wind up, close up *start, begin*; 2 whole, entire, thorough *incomplete*

complex 1 complicated, confused, involved, mixed *simple*; 2 prejudice, bias, leaning, inclination

complicate confuse, confound, involve, mix up *simplify*

compliment commend, flatter, praise, congratulate

comply conform, agree, assent, submit, obey *dissent*

compose 1 make up, devise, put together, construct, build, create, make; 2 calm, pacify, soothe, quiet

composition 1 writing, work, paper, document, script; 2 composite, combination, mixture, blend

composure calmness, quiet, self-control, peace, rest, serenity, tranquility *excitement, agitation*

comprehend 1 understand, realize, know; 2 include, contain, cover *exclude*

compress squeeze, press, reduce, condense, concentrate, crush *expand, spread*

comprise include, consist of, contain, involve *exclude*

compromise settle, yield, concede, adjust, meet halfway

compulsory compelling, required, necessary

compute calculate, count, figure, estimate, reckon

comrade friend, pal, companion, partner, chum

conceal hide, cover, cloak, veil, camouflage *disclose*

concede admit, allow, grant, confess *refuse, deny*

conceited vain, boastful, proud, cocky, saucy

conceivable imaginable, thinkable, possible, likely, plausible *inconceivable, doubtful*

concentrate   1 think about, focus   *wander (in thought)*;   2 strengthen, intensify, make stronger   *weaken*

concept   thought, notion, idea, opinion

concern   1 interest, affect, trouble, involve; 2 business, company, firm, enterprise

concert   1 music, recital;   2 agreement, harmony, unison, teamwork

conciliate   soothe, allay, quiet, calm, pacify, moderate, restrain, alleviate *antagonise, irritate*

concise   brief, short, terse, curt   *lengthy*

conclude   1 close, end, finish, stop, terminate *begin*;   2 reason, suppose, assume, presume, infer, gather

concord   peace, harmony, agreement

concrete   1 real, solid, substantial, tangible *abstract, flimsy*;   2 cement, pavement

concur   agree, cooperate   *disagree*

condemn   disapprove, doom, censure, blame, reproach, denounce, criticize   *approve*

condense   compress, squeeze, reduce, concentrate   *enlarge, expand*

condition   1 circumstance, situation, state; 2 provision, specification

conduct   1 manage, direct, guide, lead; 2 behaviour, action, manner

confederation   league, alliance, association, union

confer   consult, discuss, talk over

confess   admit, acknowledge, consent   *deny*

confide   trust in, rely, depend, tell a secret, disclose

confident   certain, sure, convinced, believing *doubtful*

confidential   secret, unpublishable, off the record

confine   enclose, surround, contain, keep in, coop up, imprison, restrain   *free, release*

confirm establish, verify, substantiate, prove

conflict 1 clash, oppose, disagree, differ *agree*; 2 fight, struggle, opposition, contest, battle *peace*

conform comply, agree, assent, submit, obey *dissent*

confound confuse, perplex, baffle, puzzle, mystify, bewilder, stump *clarify*

confront oppose, face, meet squarely, encounter

confuse complicate, mix up, mistake, muddle, jumble *clarify*

congenial agreeable, pleasing, compatible, harmonious, like-minded *conflicting*

congested overcrowded, overloaded, stuffed, full *empty*

congratulate bless, compliment, flatter, commend, praise

congregate crowd, mass, gather, meet, assemble *disperse, scatter*

conjecture guess, suppose

connect join, unite, combine, link, attach *disconnect, separate*

conquer overtake, vanquish, defeat, crush, win, triumph

conscientious exacting, particular, faithful, scrupulous *neglectful*

conscious 1 alive, awake *unconscious*; 2 knowing, realizing, sensitive, sensible, aware, cognizant *unaware*

consecutive following, successive, continuous *interrupted*

consent permit, agree, assent, accept, approve of, comply *refuse*

consequently therefore, as a result, accordingly, hence

conservative cautious, opposed to change, unextreme, protective *changing*

conserve preserve, save, keep, guard, protect, maintain

consider 1 think, study, ponder, reflect, contemplate, deliberate; 2 think of, regard, look upon

considerable important, much, great, significant, powerful *insignificant, unimportant*

considerate thoughtful, mindful of others, kind, sympathetic *inconsiderate, thoughtless*

consist comprise, make up, include

consistency 1 firmness, stiffness; 2 steadiness, uniformity *changing*

consolidate unite, combine, condense, concentrate, merge, compress, squeeze, reduce

conspicuous noticeable, distinct, clear, obvious, prominent, outstanding *inconspicuous*

conspire plot, scheme

constantly always, often, without stopping, continual *seldom, scarcely*

consternation dismay, alarm, terror, fright, scare, dread

constitute organize, form, set up, establish, compose

constrict contract, compress, squeeze, press, crush *expand, spread*

construct manufacture, form, build, make, create

constructive helpful, useful, worthwhile *destructive*

consult confer, discuss, talk over

consume 1 use up, spend, eat up, drink up; 2 waste, destroy, exhaust

contact touch, connect, reach, join, approach

contagious catching, spreading, infectious, epidemic

contain 1 hold, include, comprise, consist of, involve *exclude*; 2 control, restrain, curb

contaminate pollute, corrupt, defile, infect *purify*

contemplate 1 consider, think, study, ponder, reflect, deliberate; 2 plan, intend, expect

contemptible mean, atrocious, wicked, cruel, brutal, ruthless, terrible, horrible, dreadful, awful, vile, wretched *good, angelic*

contend fight, struggle, argue, quarrel

contented satisfied, pleased, delighted *dissatisfied*

contest 1 contend, fight, struggle, argue, quarrel; 2 game, sport, tournament

continue last, endure, go on, keep on, persist *discontinue, stop*

contortion twist, distortion, crookedness

contour outline, profile, form

contraband prohibited, forbidden, illegal, smuggled, outlawed *legal*

1. contract 1 form, start, enter into; 2 agreement, pact, understanding, bargain, treaty, alliance, deal

2. contract shrink, reduce, compress *expand*

contradict deny, oppose, dispute *agree*

contrary opposed, opposite, different, clashing, conflicting *agreeable*

contrast compare, match, liken, measure

contribute give, donate, participate, provide

contrive invent, scheme, plan, plot, devise, conspire

control 1 command, influence, master; 2 restrain, check, contain, curb

controversy dispute, argument, quarrel

convene gather, meet, assemble *disperse*

convenient handy, suitable, timely, nearby *inconvenient*

conventional customary, usual, traditional, accepted, established, formal *unusual*

converse talk, speak with, discuss, communicate with

convert change, transform

convey 1 carry, transport, take; 2 communicate, inform, tell, enlighten, report; 3 transfer, consign, hand over, deliver, entrust, send

convict condemn, doom, sentence *acquit*

convince persuade, assure, make certain, promise, guarantee, pledge

convoy accompany, escort, protect, conduct, guide, lead

convulsion fit, tantrum, seizure, spasm, attack

cool 1 chilly, fresh *warm*; 2 calm, unexcited *excited*

cooperate work together, collaborate

coordinate arrange, organize, harmonize

cope struggle, put up, face, deal with

copious plentiful, abundant, ample *scarce*

copy imitate, repeat, duplicate, reproduce

cordial sincere, hearty, warm, friendly, hospitable *unfriendly*

corporation industry, company, business, firm, enterprise

correct 1 mark, change, remedy, adjust; 2 true, right, proper, accurate *incorrect, wrong*

correspond 1 write, communicate with; 2 agree, harmonize, resemble

corroborate confirm, establish, verify, substantiate, prove, endorse

corrode deteriorate, eat away, rot, rust

corrupt wicked, evil, rotten, dishonest, crooked, shady

cost 1 price, charge, rate, amount; 2 loss, sacrifice, expense

council conference, assembly, committee, group, delegation

counsel   advise, recommend, suggest
count   1 add, total, number;   2 depend, rely;
3 consider, regard, judge
counteract   1 offset, balance, neutralize;   2 act
against, oppose, contradict, cross   *agree*
counterfeit   copied, imitation, fake, artificial
authentic, real
countless   many, endless, unlimited,
innumerable   *limited*
country   land, region, nation, territory
courage   bravery, boldness, valour, gallantry
cowardice
courier   messenger, runner
course   direction, line, way, track, channel
court   1 please, pursue, chase, woo;   2 yard,
enclosure;   3 playground, field;   4 tribunal
courteous   polite, civil, gracious, obliging,
respectful   *rude*
covenant   agreement, pact, contract,
understanding, concord, bargain, treaty,
alliance
cover   1 hide, protect, shelter, conceal
uncover;   2 include, consist of, comprise,
contain, involve   *exclude*
covert   1 secret, hidden, disguised, covered,
veiled, concealed   *open*;   2 shelter,
hiding place, hideaway, refuge
covet   desire, crave, lust, want, envy
coward   weakling   *hero, brave person*
cozy   comfortable, snug, relaxing, homely
uncomfortable
crack   1 break, split, open, slit;   2 blow, shot,
bang, noise
craft   skill, trade, art, handicraft
crafty   sly, scheming, calculating, plotting,
cunning
cramp   1 confine, box in, limit, restrict;   2 pain,
twinge

cranky cross, irritable, churlish *good-humoured*

crave covet, desire, lust, want

crazy insane, mad, lunatic, daft, unbalanced *sane*

crease fold, ridge, wrinkle, crinkle

create 1 make, form, invent, originate, manufacture; 2 cause, produce, bring about

credit belief, trust, faith

credulous undoubting, believing, trusting, gullible *doubting*

crest 1 decoration, insignia; 2 tuft, feathers, plume; 3 peak, ridge, summit, top, crown *base*

crestfallen dejected, depressed, discouraged, downcast *cheerful, merry*

crevice cleft, rift, gap, break

crew staff, force, gang

crime wrongdoing, sin, vice, evil

cripple damage, weaken, disable, injure

crisis emergency, critical point, crucial period, turning point

crisp 1 brittle, fragile, frail, breakable *strong*; 2 fresh, sharp, clear, bracing

critical 1 disapproving, faultfinding *approving*; 2 crucial, decisive, urgent, pressing *unimportant*

crook 1 hook, bend, curve; 2 criminal, gangster, lawbreaker, thief

crop 1 cut, clip, shear; 2 produce, growth, yield, harvest

cross 1 pass, step over; 2 mate, interbreed; 3 oppose, go against; 4 cranky, irritable, churlish *good-humoured*

crowd group, mass, throng, mob

crown 1 honour, reward, glorify, decorate; 2 head; 3 crest, peak, ridge, summit, top *base*; 4 head ornament, tiara

crucial important, critical, urgent, decisive, pressing *unimportant*

crucify torture, torment, punish, execute

crude rough, unrefined, raw, vulgar *refined*

cruel mean, heartless, brutal, ruthless *kind*

crumble break up, disintegrate

crusade cause, movement, drive, campaign

crush 1 subdue, conquer; 2 compress, squeeze, press, reduce *expand*

crutch support, prop, brace

cry wail, sob, weep, bawl *laugh*

cuddle snuggle, nestle, fondle

cue hint, signal, clue, key, lead

culminate top, crown, end, terminate

culpable guilty, faulty, blamable *innocent*

culprit offender, sinner, wrongdoer

cultivate condition, prepare, train, develop, improve

cultured refined, learned, polished, well-bred *uncouth*

cumbersome bulky, clumsy, awkward, unmanageable, burdensome, troublesome *manageable*

cunning skilful, clever, crafty, sly, scheming, calculating, plotting

curb check, stop, control, restrain

cure restore, remedy, heal

curious 1 strange, odd, unusual, queer, peculiar; 2 inquisitive

current 1 flow, stream; 2 prevalent, present *past*

curse 1 swear; 2 affliction, trouble, burden

curtail shorten, abbreviate, condense, abridge, contract, reduce, cut, compress *lengthen*

cushion 1 soften, support; 2 pillow

custodian guardian, keeper, caretaker

custom tradition, use, habit, practice, way, manner

cut 1 reduce, contract, abbreviate, shorten, curtail, condense, abridge, compress *increase*; 2 sever, split

cycle series, circle

D

daily regularly, day by day

damage harm, hurt, impair, spoil, ruin, upset *remedy*, *repair*

damn condemn, doom, denounce, censure, curse

dampen 1 moisten, wet, sprinkle; 2 depressed, discouraged; 3 muffle, mute, dull, deaden, smother, suppress *encourage*

dangerous unsafe, hazardous, risky, perilous, chancy *safe*

dank wet, moist, damp, humid, muggy *dry*

dapper neat, trim, smart, chic, well-dressed, natty, sporty, dressy, swanky

daring bold, fearless, audacious, foolhardy, adventurous *cautious*

dark 1 black, obscure *light*; 2 gloomy, dismal, sombre, solemn, grave, dreary *cheerful*; 3 hidden, secret, concealed, obscured *open*

data facts, information, evidence, proof, grounds

date 1 time, day; 2 appointment, engagement; 3 fruit

daub 1 grease, lubricate, coat, cover; 2 soil, dirty, stain, spot, smear; 3 scribble, scrawl, paint badly

daunt frighten, discourage, deter, dishearten *encourage*

dawn 1 daybreak, sunrise *sunset*; 2 beginning, start, commencement, outset *ending*

dazzle   shine, glow, flash, glaze, glare, blind
dead   1 lifeless, deceased, gone;   2 dull,
   inactive, flat, dreary   *alive*
deal   1 allot, grant, give;   2 trade, buy, sell;
   3 act, behave;   4 bargain, compact,
   agreement, understanding, transaction
dear   1 precious, darling, beloved, adored,
   admired, idolized;   2 expensive, costly, high-
   priced   *inexpensive, cheap*
debase   lower, discredit, degrade, demote, run
   down   *lift*
debate   discuss, argue, reason, dispute
debris   ruins, rubbish, trash, scrap, litter,
   residue, junk
debt   obligation, amount, due
decay   rot, spoil, crumble, disintegrate
   flourish, bloom
decease   die, perish, depart, expire
deceive   beguile, trick, hoax, dupe, betray,
   mislead, lie
decent   1 respectable, proper, correct, right
   improper;   2 adequate, good enough,
   suitable, fit   *inadequate*
decide   settle, determine, resolve, judge
decipher   solve, explain, figure out
declare   state, assert, announce, affirm, say,
   pronounce
decline   1 refuse, reject   *accept*;   2 sink, fail,
   run down, fall, weaken   *strengthen*;   3 slope,
   descent, slant, hill
decompose   decay, rot, crumble, disintegrate
decorate   adorn, trim, beautify, ornament, fix
   up
decoy   bait, lure
decrease   lessen, diminish, reduce, curtail, cut,
   shorten, compress   *increase*
decree   pronounce, order, rule, pass judgment,
   command, dictate

dedicate   inscribe, devote, address, assign

deduct   subtract, remove, withdraw, take away, discount   *add*

deed   1 act, action, performance, doing; 2 contract, policy

deface   mar, blemish, disfigure, deform   *improve*

defeat   overcome, win, triumph

defect   fault, flaw, weakness, failing, shortcoming, blemish, imperfection, deficiency   *perfection*

defend   protect, safeguard, shield, support   *attack*

defer   1 put off, delay, postpone; 2 yield, submit, bow to, respect, accept, acknowledge

deficient   lacking, incomplete, wanting, needing, missing   *complete*

define   1 explain, describe, clarify; 2 fix, set, establish, outline

definite   clear, precise, distinct, plain, obvious, evident, clear-cut, exact   *indefinite, unclear*

deform   disfigure, blemish, mar, spoil, make ugly   *improve, beautify*

defraud   cheat, swindle, gyp

deft   skilful, nimble, clever, adept, expert, proficient, apt, handy, ingenious   *clumsy*

defy   resist, confront, challenge, disobey, ignore, disregard   *obey*

degrade   demote, reduce, lower, downgrade

degree   1 step, grade, notch, amount, extent, measure, period; 2 rank, title, honour

deity   divinity, god

dejected   sad, depressed, discouraged, downcast, disheartened, despondent   *cheerful*

delay   detain, put off, postpone, hold up

delegate   1 assign, authorize, entrust, appoint, charge; 2 representative, envoy, agent, deputy

deliberate 1 ponder, consider, think over, study, meditate, reflect, mull over; 2 slow, leisurely, easy, unhurried *hasty*

delicate mild, soft, fine, dainty, frail, light, fragile, sensitive, tender *gross*

delightful pleasant, lovely, charming, appealing, pleasing *unpleasant*

delirious giddy, raving, frantic, mad, violent, hysterical

deliver 1 transfer, pass, hand over, consign, give; 2 say, voice, express, communicate, recite, relate; 3 free, rescue, release, liberate

delude mislead, deceive, beguile, hoax, dupe, fool, betray

deluge 1 flood, overflow, run over, overwhelm; 2 rain, flood, torrent, storm

demand 1 ask, inquire, want to know; 2 require, need, call for, want

demolish destroy, wreck, tear apart, dismantle, shatter *restore*

demonstrate display, show, illustrate, clarify

demote degrade, reduce, lower *promote*

denomination group, sect, class, kind, brand, sort, name

denote indicate, mean, say, signify, imply, show, mark, express

denounce blame, censure, reproach, condemn, accuse, charge, indict, damn *commend*

dense 1 crowded, packed, compact, thick, heavy, close, solid, compressed *empty*; 2 stupid, dull, thick *bright, smart*

deny refute, contradict, dispute, renounce, reject *admit*

depart 1 leave, go away, exit; 2 die, decease, perish, pass on *arrive*

depend rely, trust, confide

depict represent, portray, describe, picture, illustrate, characterize

deposit 1 put down, lay, place, leave, store
withdraw; 2 pledge, stake

depot 1 station, stand, post; 2 storehouse,
depository, warehouse

depress 1 sadden, deject, discourage,
dishearten *cheer*; 2 lower, sink *raise*;
3 weaken, reduce, lessen *increase*

deprive take away, take from *give*

deride ridicule, laugh at, make fun of

derive get, obtain, acquire, gain, secure,
receive

derogatory belittling, unfavourable,
slanderous *flattering*

descend decline, fall, drop, plunge *ascend*

describe define, characterize, portray, picture,
depict, represent, paint, tell

desert leave, forsake, abandon

deserve merit, earn, be worthy of

design 1 sketch, draw, paint, picture, portray,
depict; 2 intend, plan, propose

designate 1 show, indicate, point out, specify;
2 name, nominate, appoint

desire wish, want, fancy, lust

desist stop, cease, end, halt, discontinue,
abandon *continue*

desolate 1 empty, vacant, void, barren
dense; 2 gloomy, dismal, dreary *cheerful*

despair lose hope, give up

desperate frantic, wild, reckless, mad

despise hate, scorn, loathe, disdain *love*

despondent depressed, dejected, downhearted,
downcast, discouraged *cheerful*

destination 1 end, goal, objective; 2 lot,
fortune, fate

destitute poor, penniless, bankrupt,
down-and-out *wealthy*

destroy 1 spoil, ruin, wreck, devastate
restore; 2 kill, slay, exterminate, finish

detach 1 separate, unfasten, disconnect *join, attach*; 2 assign, delegate, draft

detail 1 itemize, elaborate, dwell on, tell fully; 2 commission, assign, delegate; 3 part, portion, fraction, division, segment, fragment

detain delay, retard, hold up, slow up *hurry*

detect discover, spot, spy, recognize, perceive, catch

deter discourage, hinder, prevent, prohibit *encourage*

determined firm, sure, convinced, resolute, resolved, serious *doubtful*

detest hate, dislike, loathe, abhor, despise, scorn *love*

detour shift, go around, bypass

devastate destroy, ruin, wreck

develop 1 grow, flourish, mature; 2 progress, advance

device 1 machine, apparatus, tool, instrument, implement; 2 plan, scheme, trick

devil demon, fiend, ogre, monster

devise plan, invent, contrive, arrange, create, make up

devote dedicate, assign, apply, attend to

devotion 1 affection, love, fondness, liking *hatred*; 2 loyalty, dedication *infidelity*

devout 1 religious, pious; 2 earnest, sincere, hearty, devoted, serious, zealous *indifferent*

dexterity skill, cleverness, competence

diagnose interpret, gather, deduce, analyze

diagram draw, sketch, portray, design, depict

dialogue conversation, talk, speech, words

diary record book, memo, journal, account, chronicle

dice 1 cube, cut; 2 cubes

dictate 1 order, demand, direct, instruct, rule, charge; 2 read aloud

die decrease, perish, expire, pass away *live*

different unlike, distinct, opposite, contrary, reverse, dissimilar, varied, assorted *same, alike*

difficult hard, rough, rugged, arduous *easy*

dig scoop, excavate, gouge, tunnel

digest 1 absorb; 2 understand, comprehend, grasp, catch on; 3 brief, summary

digit 1 number, numeral, figure; 2 finger or toe

dignified noble, worthy, stately, majestic, grand *undignified*

dilapidated decayed, ruined, battered, broken-down, rundown

dilate expand, enlarge, widen, broaden, magnify, increase *contract, reduce*

diligent hard-working, industrious, energetic *lazy*

dilute weaken, reduce, thin, cut, water down *strengthen*

dim faint, weak, pale, indistinct, vague, darkish *bright*

dimension measurement, size, expanse, proportions

diminish decrease, reduce, lessen, curtail, cut *increase, enlarge*

din noise, racket, clamour, uproar, tumult *quiet*

dingy dirty, dull, grimy, dark, grey *bright*

diplomat politician, envoy, ambassador, emissary, a tactful person

direct 1 manage, control, conduct, handle, head, govern, rule, regulate; 2 order, command, dictate, instruct, charge; 3 show, point, aim; 4 address, inscribe

dirty grimy, soiled, muddy, untidy, dingy, messy, sloppy *clean*

disable cripple, make useless, put out of order, weaken

disadvantage drawback, handicap, liability, inconvenience *advantage*

disagree differ, quarrel, conflict, dispute *agree*

disappear vanish, go away, fade out *appear*

disappoint dissatisfy, let down, displease *satisfy*

disapprove disfavour, frown upon, object to, oppose *approve*

disarm demilitarize, paralyse, make powerless *strengthen*

disaster casualty, calamity, misfortune, mishap, catastrophe, tragedy, accident *good fortune*

disband separate, scatter, disperse, split, break up, dismiss, dissolve *assemble*

discard reject, throw away, get rid of, dispose of, scrap, cast off *keep*

discern see, behold, observe, view, perceive, recognize, know, realize, understand, detect, spot, spy

discharge unload, release, dismiss, expel, dump, fire, let go

disciple believer, follower, convert

discipline 1 train, drill, exercise, practise, prepare, condition, groom; 2 punish, chastise, correct, penalize

disclaim deny, refuse, withhold, reject *accept*

disclose uncover, open, reveal, show, expose, unmask *hide, conceal*

discomfort distress, trouble, bother, disturb, perturb, upset *comfort, please*

discord 1 disagreement, difference, dispute, conflict, friction *agreement*; 2 noise, racket, din, clamour *quiet*

discount 1 deduct, subtract, remove *add*; 2 allow for, consider, take into account

discourage deter, prevent, hinder, disapprove,

keep from, deject, daunt *encourage*

discover reveal, learn, observe, see, notice, perceive, find, disclose, expose

discredit 1 doubt, disbelieve *believe*; 2 disgrace, dishonour, shame, humiliate

discreet careful, prudent, considerate, thoughtful, cautious *indiscreet*

discriminate separate, segregate, distinguish, set apart

discuss debate, talk over, reason, consider, confer

disdain scorn, despise, reject, spurn *respect*

disease sickness, illness, ailment, malady, infirmity *health*

disfigure deform, deface, blemish, mar, injure, scar, spoil

disgrace shame, dishonour, discredit, humiliate, embarrass

disguise conceal, hide, cover, camouflage, misrepresent

disgust sicken, offend, repel, revolt, nauseate

dishearten discourage, depress, sadden, deject *cheer*

dishevelled rumpled, untidy, sloppy *neat*

disintegrate break up, separate, decompose, crumble, decay, rot

dismal dark, gloomy, dreary, miserable, bleak, depressing *bright, cheerful*

dismantle disassemble, take apart, demolish, wreck

dismay bewilder, disturb, embarrass, bother, confuse, alarm, frighten

dismiss discharge, expel, send away *enlist*

dispatch 1 send, transmit, forward, discharge; 2 hurry, hasten, speed, rush

dispel scatter, disperse, drive away *assemble*

dispense distribute, give out, deal out, issue, allot, grant, dole out, mete out

disperse scatter, distribute, spread

display demonstrate, illustrate, exhibit, present, parade, flaunt *conceal*

disposal 1 removal, elimination, release; 2 arrangement, settlement, adjustment, administration

disposition 1 nature, temperament, character, inclination; 2 arrangement, settlement, order, adjustment, administration

dispute argue, debate, quarrel, oppose, resist, fight, bicker, contest *agree*

dissect cut, examine, analyze

dissent disagree, differ, take exception *agree*

dissipate 1 scatter, spread, dispel, disperse; 2 squander, waste, spend foolishly *save*

dissolve 1 melt, liquidize; 2 cease, end, fade, pass away, disappear

dissuade discourage, talk out of *persuade*

distance 1 space, length, extent, reach; 2 far away *nearness*

distend expand, swell, stretch, widen, enlarge, magnify, increase, blow out, bulge *contract, decrease*

distinct 1 different, dissimilar, diverse, separate, similar; 2 clear, plain, obvious, precise, exact, clear-cut, definite, unmistakable *indefinite*

distinguish 1 tell apart, define, see, detect; 2 honour, dignify, make famous

distinguished important, great, outstanding, famous, well-known, noted, popular, celebrated, honoured

distract divert, confuse, disturb

distress pain, hurt, afflict, torment, torture, agonize, trouble, bother, disturb, upset *please*

distribute scatter, disperse, spread, dispense, allot, dole out, mete out *collect*

district   region, area, zone, territory, place, section, neighbourhood

disturb   1 annoy, irk, vex, bother, irritate; 2 trouble, perturb, concern, agitate, upset, excite, alarm

dive   plunge, drop, fall

diverse   1 different, unlike, distinct; 2 various, several *same*

divert   1 distract, detract, confuse; 2 amuse, entertain, delight, tickle

divide   separate, portion, partition, split, share, sort *unite*

divine   1 heavenly, sacred, holy; 2 superb, delightful, excellent, great, beautiful; 3 foretell, predict, guess, forecast, prophesy, anticipate

divorce   separate, disjoin, divide, disconnect

divulge   reveal, tell, make known, publish, broadcast, circulate, let out, come out with

dizzy   giddy, staggering, spinning, unsteady, confused *steady*

do   perform, act, behave, produce

docile   obedient, willing, receptive, responsive, yielding, gentle, tame, mild *stubborn*

doctrine   belief, teachings, creed

document   writing, paper, certificate, statements

dodge   avoid, duck, recoil

dogged   stubborn, wilful, headstrong, obstinate *yielding*

doldrums   blues, low spirits, gloom *cheerfulness*

dole   give, donate, allot, dispense, grant, deal out, mete out

domain   sphere, realm, province, field, property

domestic   1 household, family, internal; 2 tame; 3 servant, maid

dominate   control, rule, command, lead

dominion　1 rule, control, command, power, hold, grasp;　2 lands, sphere, country, domain

donate　give, contribute, present, bestow, award, allot, grant

done　finished, complete, ended, concluded, terminated, over, wound up, through with

dormant　sleeping, inactive　*active, awake*

dose　amount, quantity, portion

double　1 duplicate, copy;　2 fold, turn over;　3 twice as much

doubt　mistrust, suspect, question, challenge, dispute　*believe*

dowdy　shabby, untidy, old-fashioned, seedy　*smart*

downcast　dejected, sad, discouraged, disheartened, depressed, gloomy, melancholy, glum　*cheerful*

downfall　1 ruin, failure, defeat, upset, overthrow　*success*;　2 rainstorm, cloudburst, flood, downpour

downpour　rainstorm, cloudburst, flood, downfall

downright　thorough, complete, plain, positive, utter, absolute, entire, total

dowry　1 settlement, endowment;　2 talent, gift, ability, genius

drab　dull, unattractive, flat, lifeless　*bright*

draft　1 sketch, drawing, rough copy, outline;　2 enlistment, enrolment, induction, call-up, recruitment;　3 note, bill, check

drag　1 pull, heave, haul, draw, tug, tow;　2 crawl, creep, linger on, tarry, lag, dillydally, delay　*speed*

drain　1 dry, empty, draw off;　2 deprive, filter, use, spend, exhaust　*replenish*

dramatize　stage, produce, present, feature, put on

drastic extreme, severe, intense, rough, violent, fierce, tough *mild*

draw 1 pull, drag, haul; 2 attract, lure, magnetize, interest *repel*; 3 sketch, portray, picture, design; 4 tie, equal, match

drawback disadvantage, handicap, fault, obstacle, objection, failing, shortcoming, flaw, catch *advantage*

dread fear, be afraid

dreadful bad, terrible, awful, unpleasant, horrible, vile, wretched, detestable, ghastly *splendid*

dream imagine, vision, muse

dreary gloomy, dull, dismal, sombre, depressing, discouraging, disheartening *pleasant*

dredge dig, excavate, scoop, pick up

dress clothe, adorn, decorate, attire, outfit

dressing 1 medicine, bandage; 2 sauce, seasoning

dribble drip, trickle, leak

drift wander, roam, stray, meander, ramble, float, cruise, glide

drill 1 practise, instruct, teach, train, exercise, prepare, condition, discipline; 2 tool

drink swallow, sip, quaff, gulp

drive 1 steer, ride, handle, operate, work, run, conduct, manage; 2 move, thrust, compel, force, make, impel

drizzle rain, shower, sprinkle

drool salivate, dribble, trickle

droop 1 hang, dangle, drag; 2 weaken, sink, fade, fail, decline; 3 despond, despair, lose heart, give up

drop 1 fall, dive, plunge, descend *rise*; 2 end, cease, stop *start*; 3 dismiss, let go, give up, abandon; 4 hardly anything, small amount *much*

drown submerge, sink, immerse, inundate
drowsy sleepy, dreamy, heavy-eyed *awake, alert*
drudge work away, plod
drug 1 numb, deaden, put to sleep, knock out;
2 medicine, potion, narcotic
drunk intoxicated, tipsy, dizzy
dual twofold, double, duplicate
dub name, call, title, label, tag, christen
dubious doubtful, uncertain, questionable
certain
duck 1 plunge, dip, submerge, sink, immerse,
dunk; 2 sidestep; 3 web-footed bird
due 1 proper, rightful, fitting, just, fair, square,
equitable *unfair*; 2 owed, *paid*
duel fight, contest, contend, struggle
dull 1 blunt, unsharp *sharp*; 2 grey, dingy,
dreary *bright*; 3 stupid, slow *clever*;
4 boring, uninteresting, dry, flat
interesting; 5 slow, inactive, sluggish *busy*
dumb 1 silent, mute, speechless; 2 stupid,
dull, dense *smart*
dump empty, unload, discharge, discard, throw
away, scrap
dupe deceive, trick, beguile, betray, hoax,
bamboozle
duplicate copy, repeat, reproduce, double
durable longlasting, enduring, permanent,
endless, sturdy, solid, strong *perishable*
duration time, period, term
dusk 1 sundown, sunset, twilight, evening,
nightfall *dawn*; 2 shade, dark, gloom
dust 1 clean, wipe off; 2 sprinkle, powder;
3 fine powder
duty 1 task, work, job, chore, assignment,
charge, function, obligation, responsibility;
2 tax, toll, tariff
dwell live, reside, inhabit, occupy

dwindle shrink, decrease, diminish, lessen, decline, subside, waste away *increase*

dye colour, stain, tint

dynamic active, energetic, forceful, strong, lively, intense, animated, spirited *weak*

E

eager wanting, wishing, desirous, anxious, keen, ready, willing *unconcerned*

earn get, gain, obtain, require, secure, make, deserve, merit, be in line for

earnest determined, sincere, serious, decided, resolute, devoted *insecure*

earth 1 world, globe; 2 ground, dirt, soil, land, sod

ease 1 relieve, reduce, soothe, allay, comfort, lighten, relax, loosen *aggravate*; 2 help, aid, facilitate

easy 1 simple, effortless, plain, not hard *hard*; 2 comfortable, restful, relaxing, cozy, snug *uncomfortable*; 3 kindly, mild, gentle, lenient *strict*; 4 pleasant, smooth, natural, informal *formal*

eat 1 dine, consume, chew, swallow; 2 corrode, erode, waste away

ebb decrease, diminish, lessen, decline, subside, recede, retreat, withdraw *increase*

eccentric unusual, peculiar, odd, abnormal, irregular, queer *normal*

echo repeat, duplicate, imitate

eclipse hide, conceal, cover, screen, veil, obscure, darken, shadow, overcast

economy thrift, frugality, saving

ecstasy joy, rapture, happiness, delight, glee, elation *sadness*

edge border, bound, fringe

edict decree, order, law, ruling, proclamation

edit   correct, check, rewrite, revise, amend

educate   teach, instruct, school, train, tutor, enlighten, direct, guide, show

effect   cause, influence, produce, bring about, evoke, determine, achieve, make, accomplish, execute, complete

effort   attempt, try, endeavour, undertaking

eject   remove, eliminate, drive out, expel, oust *receive, include*

elaborate   dwell on, develop, work out, detail

elapse   pass, expire, run out, slip away

elastic   1 flexible, pliable, yielding, adaptable *inflexible*;   2 rubber band

elated   overjoyed, enchanted, delighted, jubilant, rejoicing   *unhappy*

elder   older, senior   *younger*

elect   choose, pick, select, vote for, appoint

elegant   refined, superior, tasteful, polished, cultured, fine   *vulgar*

elementary   fundamental, basic, primary, essential, simple, beginning, introductory, initial, underlying   *advanced*

elevate   lift, raise, boost

eligible   qualified, fit, desirable, suitable *ineligible*

eliminate   remove, discard, reject, throw out, get rid of, exclude, dispose of   *include*

eloquent   fluent, well-spoken, expressive, meaningful

else   other, different, instead, another

elude   avoid, escape, evade, miss, dodge

emaciated   thin, undernourished, wasted, starved, haggard

emancipate   free, release, liberate, deliver, rescue, save   *enslave, restrain*

embalm   preserve, keep

embankment   bank, buttress, shore, barrier, dam, fortification

embark depart, start, board *disembark*

embarrass fluster, confuse, bewilder, humiliate, shame, mortify

embed enclose, fix, root, plant, lodge, wedge, inset, inlay

embezzle steal, thieve, take, rob

embitter anger, provoke, incense, arouse, inflame, antagonize, alienate, set against

emblem symbol, sign, token, badge, mark

embody include, comprise, contain, cover, take in, embrace, incorporate *exclude*

embrace 1 grasp, hug, clasp, enfold, press, hold, clutch; 2 include, contain, comprise, cover, involve; 3 accept, adopt, take up

embroider 1 stitch, decorate, ornament, adorn, trim, embellish; 2 exaggerate, overstate, overdo, stretch, magnify

emerge appear, come out, come into view

emergency crisis, crucial, period, pinch

emigrate leave, migrate

eminent high, great, prominent, noble, distinguished, superior, important, outstanding, famous *unknown*

emissary delegate, messenger, envoy, agent, diplomat, minister, ambassador, spy

emit give off, discharge, ooze, send out *receive*

emotion feeling, sentiment, sensitivity, excitement

emphasis stress, importance, accent, insistence

employ hire, engage, contract, sign, retain, occupy, busy, use

empower permit, enable, authorize, sanction, license, warrant, commission, delegate, assign, entrust

empty 1 discharge, let out, eliminate, evacuate; 2 flow out, drain, run out; 3 vacant, void, barren, blank *full*

emulate imitate, follow, copy, rival, vie with, compete with

enable empower, qualify, authorize, sanction, license *forbid*

enact 1 pass, legislate; 2 portray, represent, act out, perform, stage

encircle include, take in, comprise, enclose, surround, encompass, bound

enclose surround, fence, contain, include, encircle, envelop, shut in

encompass encircle, include, surround, cnclose

encounter 1 meet, come across; 2 battle, confront, collide, oppose

encourage support, urge, invite, promote, sponsor, cheer, inspire *discourage*

encroach intrude, interfere, infringe, trespass, break in upon

encumber burden, load, weigh down, hamper, saddle with *relieve*

end finish, stop, terminate, close, conclude, cease, quit, discontinue, halt, result, complete, wind up, clean up

endanger risk, imperil, jeopardize, hazard

endear charm, captivate, allure

endeavour try, effort, strive, attempt, labour, struggle

endless continuous, constant, ceaseless, incessant, uninterrupted, nonstop, eternal, infinite, perpetual, everlasting

endorse sign, approve, support, accept, ratify, certify, confirm, validate, pass

endow give, invest, bequeath, provide, supply, furnish, contribute

endure 1 last, continue, persist, remain, stay *vanish*; 2 stand, undergo, bear, experience, feel, suffer, tolerate

enemy opponent, foe, opposition *friend, ally*

energy   force, strength, vigour, potency, vim, drive, might, power, vitality, stamina *weakness*

enforce   compel, force, make, oblige, drive, execute

engage   1 involve, entangle, absorb, engross, occupy, hold, grip;   2 employ, busy, hire, contract for;   3 promise, agree, commit

engaging   interesting, absorbing, fascinating, engrossing, enthralling, spellbinding, charming, enchanting, captivating, appealing, tempting, enticing, delightful, lovely, exquisite   *dull, boring*

engender   cause, produce, develop, generate, breed

engineer   guide, manage, direct, regulate, conduct, run, lead, manoeuvre

engrave   carve, cut, fix, print, inscribe, stamp, sketch, impress

engross   occupy, absorb, engage, fascinate, enthrall

engulf   swallow, devour, flood, inundate

enhance   improve, better, enrich, uplift *impair*

enigma   riddle, puzzle, mystery, problem, stumper

enjoy   like, appreciate, savour, relish   *dislike*

enlighten   clarify, inform, instruct, illuminate, explain, simplify, acquaint, teach, educate

enlist   1 join, enrol, sign up;   2 induce, move, influence, sway, persuade

enliven   stimulate, inspire, cheer, brighten *calm*

enmity   hate, dislike, loathing, unfriendliness *friendship*

enormous   large, great, vast, immense, huge, colossal, giant   *tiny*

enough   sufficient, ample, plenty, satisfactory, adequate   *insufficient*

enrage madden, infuriate, anger, inflame, provoke

enrich improve, enhance, better, uplift

enrol 1 list, register, write, record, join; 2 enlist, draft, induct, recruit

ensign 1 flag, banner, pennant, standard, colours; 2 officer

ensue follow, succeed, result

ensure 1 assure, make certain, guarantee, warrant, settle

entangle involve, complicate, confuse, trap, snare

enter go into, set foot in, join *exit*

enterprise ambition, project, feat, undertaking, business, venture, deed, exploit, achievement, adventure

entertain 1 amuse, delight, interest, excite, fascinate, give a party; 2 consider, contemplate, have in mind

enthusiastic interested, attracted, eager, keen about *unconcerned, uninterested*

entice attract, tempt, lure, seduce

entirely wholly, fully, altogether, completely, thoroughly, totally, exclusively, solely *partly*

entitle name, call, designate, tag, label, title, identify, authorize, empower, enable, license *forbid*

entrance 1 fascinate, charm, intrigue, enthral, enchant, delight, thrill; 2 hypnotize, spellbind; 3 entry, way in

entreat beg, ask, implore, plead

entrust delegate, assign, charge, commission

enumerate list, count, tally, number

enunciate speak, pronounce, announce, state, express

envelop wrap, cover, embrace, surround, encompass, hide, conceal

environment surroundings, neighbourhood, vicinity, setting

envoy messenger, delegate, agent, diplomat

envy covet, be jealous of

epidemic widespread, prevalent, contagious, infectious, catching

episode occurrence, happening, experience, event, incident, affair

epoch era, period, age

equal match, rival, tie, parallel *unequal*

equilibrium balance, stability, firmness, soundness, steadiness *instability*

equip provide, furnish, fit, prepare, rig, costume

equitable fair, just, square, even, rightful, due, fit, proper

equivalent equal, match, like, rival, substitute, replacement

era epoch, period, age

eradicate eliminate, get rid of, remove, exterminate

erase cancel, wipe out, obliterate, cross off

erect 1 build, construct, make rise; 2 upright, vertical, straight *bent*

erode disintegrate, break up, corrode, wear away, rust

errand task, job, chore, assignment, duty, exercise

erratic uncertain, irregular, queer, abnormal, unusual, changeable, unstable *constant*

erroneous mistaken, incorrect, untrue, wrong, false *true*

erupt burst forth, vomit, discharge, pour out

escape evade, get away, flee

escort accompany, conduct, guide, lead, usher, attend, squire, chaperon

especially particularly, principally, chiefly, mainly, mostly, primarily

essay 1 try, attempt, test, experiment, undertake; 2 composition, article, study, paper, thesis

essence 1 meaning, significance, substance; 2 perfume, scent, smell, odour, fragrance

essential needed, necessary, important, vital, fundamental, required, basic

establish 1 fix, set, settle, found, organize; 2 prove, demonstrate, show

estate property, land

esteem 1 think, consider, judge, regard; 2 prize, value, appreciate, treasure, rate highly

estimate judge, calculate, evaluate, rate, value, figure, compute, gauge

etch engrave, imprint, stamp, impress

eternal always, forever, endless, perpetual, everlasting, permanent, infinite, continual, constant, ceaseless *temporary*

etiquette manners, social code, formalities

evacuate leave, withdraw, remove, depart, quit, empty, abandon, vacate *arrive*

evade avoid, escape, miss, bypass

evaporate vanish, disappear, fade away

even 1 level, flat, smooth *uneven*; 2 same, uniform, equal, identical; 3 still, yet

evening nightfall, sunset, sundown *morning*

event happening, occurrence, incident, episode, experience

eventually finally, ultimately, in time

everlasting perpetual, permanent, eternal, infinite, endless, continual, constant, ceaseless *temporary*

every each, all

evict expel, oust, turn out

evidence facts, proof, grounds, data, indication, sign, clue

evident clear, plain, apparent, obvious, clear-cut *doubtful, vague*

evil bad, wrong, sinful, wicked *good*

evoke bring forth, summon, induce, prompt

evolve unfold, develop, grow, progress, advance

exact detailed, precise, correct, accurate *vague*

exaggerate overstate, stretch, overdo, magnify, enlarge *minimize*

examine 1 inspect, observe, study, consider, review, analyze; 2 test, quiz, question

example 1 sample, model, pattern, representative, symbol; 2 arithmetic problem

exasperate irritate, annoy, anger, infuriate, madden

excavate dig, scoop, pull up, unearth, burrow

exceed surpass, better, excel, top, cap, beat

excel surpass, better, top, cap, beat, exceed

except 1 excluding, omitting, leaving out, barring, besides, save, outside of, aside from *including*; 2 reject, exclude, deny *accept, include*

exceptional unusual, extraordinary, remarkable, notable, outstanding *ordinary*

excess left over, addition, extra, surplus, remaining *lack*

exchange change, substitute, switch, trade, swap

excite arouse, stir, stimulate, provoke, incite, move, affect *compose, calm*

exclaim cry out, clamour, shout

exclude bar, shut out, outlaw, keep out, reject, forbid, prohibit *include*

excursion trip, journey, outing, tour

excuse 1 pardon, forgive, absolve; 2 reason, alibi

execute 1 do, perform, complete, carry out, put into effect, accomplish; 2 put to death, kill

executive   directing, managing, administrative

exempt   free, release, excuse, except, let off
liable

exercise   practise, use, train, drill, prepare,
condition, perform

exert   use, employ, put forth, utilize

exhale   breathe out, give off, expel, blow
inhale

exhaust   1 empty, drain, use up, consume,
finish, spend   *save*;   2 tire, fatigue, wear out,
knock out

exhibit   show, demonstrate, display, present

exhilarate   cheer, gladden, enliven, encourage,
inspire, stimulate, refresh, excite   *sadden*,
deject

exile   banish, expel, cast out, deport, ban,
exclude   *admit*

exist   1 be, live;   2 occur, prevail

exit   depart, go out, leave   *enter*

exodus   departure, leaving, going, parting,
exit   *entrance*

exorbitant   excessive, unreasonable,
outrageous, overpriced   *cheap*

exotic   1 foreign, strange   *native*;   2 colourful,
bright, rich, vivid, gay   *dull*

expand   spread, swell, unfold, grow, enlarge,
extend, broaden, increase, magnify   *contract*,
reduce

expect   anticipate, look for, await, think,
suppose, hope

expedient   useful, helpful, fitting, desirable,
appropriate, wise, sensible   *unwise*, *absurd*

expedition   1 journey, trip, trek, pilgrimage;
2 speed, promptness, swiftness, haste, hurry
delay

expel   remove, get rid of, eliminate, eject,
dispose of, dismiss, discharge, oust, banish,
outlaw   *admit*

expend spend, use up, consume, exhaust, waste *store*

expensive costly, high-priced, dear *cheap*

experience 1 happening, occurrence, incident, episode, adventure; 2 sensation, feeling, emotion; 3 practice, knowledge, know-how *inexperience*

experiment try, test, prove, verify

expert skilful, adept, apt, handy, clever, proficient, masterful, ingenious *incompetent*

expire end, cease, perish, die, pass away, vanish, disappear *continue, commence*

explain solve, answer, clarify, simplify, illustrate, show, demonstrate

explicit clear, distinct, definite, direct, candid, express, positive, unmistakable *indefinite, unclear*

explode blow up, burst, erupt

exploit 1 use unfairly, take advantage of; 2 deed, feat, adventure, bold act

explore search, hunt, look, research, examine, investigate, delve into, probe

export send abroad, ship *import*

expose open, uncover, show, display, reveal, disclose, unmask *hide, conceal*

express 1 say, voice, present, tell, describe; 2 show, indicate, imply; 3 send, dispatch, ship; 4 fast, quick, speedy, rapid, swift *slow*

expulsion removal, ejection, elimination, discharge *admittance*

exquisite 1 lovely, delicate, beautiful, superb, magnificent, marvellous, wonderful, delightful, charming, appealing, enchanting, heavenly, attractive *ugly*; 2 sharp, intense, acute *dull*

extend 1 stretch, reach out, lengthen, increase, enlarge, expand, broaden, magnify *decrease,* *shorten*; 2 give, grant, donate, present, allot, contribute, supply, provide, furnish *take*

exterior outside, outer, external, surface *interior*

exterminate destroy, get rid of, eliminate, kill, dispose of, wipe out

external outside, outer, exterior, surface *internal*

extinct dead, gone, past, obsolete

extinguish put out, smother, quench, suppress, crush

extra additional, supplementary, surplus, more, spare

extraordinary special, unusual, remarkable, exceptional, wonderful, marvellous, noteworthy, memorable *ordinary*

extravagant extreme, excessive, overdone, exaggerated, unreasonable, luxurious, grand *meagre*

extreme 1 extravagant, excessive, exaggerated, overdone, drastic, radical *moderate*; 2 final, last, conclusive, terminal *first, beginning*

extricate release, free, liberate, rescue, clear *capture*

exult rejoice, delight, be glad *lament, grieve*

F

fable story, legend, myth, fairy tale, fiction *truth*

fabric cloth, textile, goods, material

fabulous unbelievable, amazing, remarkable, striking, notable, marvellous

facade front, face

face 1 confront, oppose, meet, encounter, brave *avoid*; 2 features, looks, countenance; 3 look, expression

facet side, aspect, view, phase

facilitate ease, help, assist, speed, smooth the
way

fact detail, item, point, truth, certainty,
evidence, data, clue *lie*

factor cause, element, part, ingredient, basis

factory plant, works

faculty 1 talent, gift, power, ability, capacity,
qualification, aptitude; 2 teachers, staff

fade 1 dim, lose colour, pale, dull, bleach;
2 weaken, sink, fail, droop, decline

fail 1 flunk, be unsuccessful, lose out
succeed; 2 neglect, fall short; 3 weaken,
fade

faint 1 swoon, black-out, weaken, keel over;
2 weak, dim, pale, indistinct, vague, hazy,
blurred *clear, strong*

fair 1 light, pale, whitish *dark*; 2 clear,
sunny, bright, pleasant *cloudy*; 3 average,
mediocre *outstanding*; 4 honest, just,
square, right, impartial *unfair, unjust*;
5 festival, fête, affair, bazaar, exposition,
market

faith 1 trust, belief, confidence, hope;
2 religion, teaching

fake 1 pretend, deceive, falsify, disguise,
distort, feign; 2 false, mock, make-believe,
imitation, counterfeit, artificial, fraudulent
real, genuine

fall 1 drop, plunge, descent, tumble *ascend*;
2 lapse, slip; 3 ruin, destruction, defeat,
overthrow; 4 autumn

false 1 untrue, incorrect, lying, wrong *true*;
2 deceitful, disloyal, two-faced *loyal*;
3 artificial, fake, counterfeit, mock,
imitation *real, genuine*

falter hesitate, stumble, stagger, waver,
flounder

fame reputation, name, renown, glory, popularity, notoriety

familiar 1 well-known, popular *unknown*; 2 friendly, close, personal, intimate *distant*; 3 well acquainted, informed in, versed in, knowledgeable *unfamiliar*

family group, household, kin, relatives, folks

famine starvation, lack, need, want, shortage, deficiency, absence *sufficiency, plenty*

fan 1 stir, arouse, whip, stimulate, spread, flare *soothe, calm*; 2 blower; 3 admirer, follower, devotee, fancier

fanatic enthusiast, zealot

fancy 1 imagine, visualize, picture, dream, suppose, think; 2 like, care for, love *dislike*; 3 elaborate, ornate, flowery, fussy, frilly *simple*

fantastic odd, unreal, strange, wild, unusual, incredible, outrageous *ordinary, usual*

fantasy 1 imagination, vision, illusion, fancy; 2 fiction, myth, fable, legend, story, fairy tale

far distant, remote, removed *near*

farm 1 cultivate, grow, raise, ranch, harvest; 2 hire, let, rent, lease, charter; 3 plantation, ranch, homestead

fascinate interest, excite, attract, enthrall, captivate, charm, intrigue, enchant, thrill, delight *bore*

fashion 1 make, shape, form, create, mould; 2 style, mode, vogue, custom

fast 1 go hungry, starve *eat*; 2 speedy, swift, rapid, quick, hasty *slow*; 3 firm, stable, sure, dependable, solid, steady *changing*

fastidious particular, selective, critical, choosy

fat 1 stout, fleshy, plump, chubby, tubby, chunky *thin*; 2 oil, lubrication, grease

fatal 1 deadly, destructive, killing, mortal, disastrous; 2 important, fateful, serious, significant *unimportant*

fate fortune, destiny, lot, end

fathom 1 understand, follow, grasp, comprehend; 2 measure, gauge

fatigue tire, exhaust, wear out

fault mistake, error, defect, flaw, shortcoming, wrongdoing, misdeed, catch

favour 1 prefer, rather, like better; 2 resemble, look like; 3 kindness, service, good deed, benefit, courtesy

favourite choice, cherished, prized, beloved, precious, pet, adored, treasured

fear dread, be afraid

feasible possible, practical, workable, attainable *impossible*

feature 1 show, headline, star; 2 part, characteristic, trait, mark

fee charge, dues, toll, fare

feeble weak, powerless, frail *strong*

feed 1 nourish, supply, nurture; 2 eat, dine

feel 1 touch, finger, handle; 2 be, seem, look, appear; 3 experience, know, encounter, meet, undergo, endure, suffer, sense

felicity 1 happiness, bliss, gladness, delight, joy, cheer, glee, enchantment; 2 blessing, good fortune, luck

fen marsh, swamp

fence 1 enclose, wall, fortify, blockade; 2 fight, joust, duel; 3 sell illegally, black-market, bootleg

ferment 1 change chemically, sour; 2 excite, agitate, disturb, stir, trouble, ruffle *calm, pacify*

ferocious fierce, savage, vicious, brutal, wild, cruel, ruthless, bloodthirsty *gentle, tame*

ferry 1 carry, transport, haul, cart; 2 boat

figure 75

fertile productive, fruitful, enriched, abundant, creative *unproductive, barren*

fervent sincere, devoted, ardent, zealous, passionate, intense, enthusiastic

fetching enchanting, appealing, interesting, enticing, inviting, alluring, fascinating, captivating, delightful, exquisite, lovely *displeasing*

fête festival, party, gala affair

feud quarrel, dispute, controversy, fight, squabble, animosity,bitterness *peace*

fever heat, flush, sickness, high body temperature

few not many, small number, very little *many*

fickle changing, unstable, not constant, flighty, uncertain, unreliable, unfaithful *constant*

fiction fantasy, untruth, invention, legend, myth, fable, fairy tale *truth, fact*

fidelity 1 loyalty, faithfulness, allegiance, devotion, faith, attachment, fealty *disloyalty*; 2 accuracy, exactness, correctness, precision

fidget fuss, twitch, jerk, wriggle, squirm, twist, wiggle

field 1 land, space, region, tract, plot, ground, pasture; 2 sphere, range, realm, area

fierce savage, raging, wild, violent, vicious, brutal, ferocious, cruel *calm, kind*

fiery 1 hot, burning, flaming; 2 aroused, excited, violent, heated, ardent, feverish, fervent *unemotional*

fight quarrel, struggle, combat, contest, battle, contend, oppose, attack, row

figure 1 symbol, number, numeral, digit; 2 price, cost, charge, amount; 3 shape, form, physique, build, structure; 4 person, individual; 5 picture, drawing, diagram, illustration, design, pattern, outline, chart, sketch

file 1 sort, classify, group, categorize,
catalogue, store; 2 march, parade;
3 smooth, grind, sand, sharpen, edge

fill 1 load, pack, stuff, cram *empty*; 2 supply,
provide, furnish

film 1 photograph, take a picture; 2 coat,
coating, layer, covering

filter strain, percolate, screen, sift, refine,
purify, cleanse, drain, separate

filth dirt, muck, foul matter, rot

final last, deciding, closing, terminal,
conclusive *beginning*

finale end, finish, conclusion, termination
beginning, opening

finance sponsor, back, support, aid, assist,
subsidize, stake

find 1 discover, disclose, come upon *lose*;
2 learn, get, gain knowledge, gather;
3 decide, declare, determine

fine 1 penalize, tax, charge; 2 delicate,
minute *coarse*; 3 refined, tasteful,
polished; 4 excellent, good, nice, splendid

finger 1 touch, handle, feel, manipulate;
2 digit

finish 1 end, complete, close, terminate,
conclude, stop, cease *begin*; 2 perfect,
polish, refine

fire 1 ignite, heat, kindle; 2 dismiss, discharge,
expel, lay off, release *hire*; 3 arouse, excite,
inflame, stir, provoke, agitate *calm,
soothe*; 4 shoot, discharge, blast

firm 1 solid, fixed, secure, unyielding,
inflexible, stationary, immovable, rigid
flexible; 2 company, business, enterprise

first 1 principal, main, chief, leading, primary,
dominant; 2 beginning, foremost, before,
ahead, in front *last*; 3 rather, sooner,
preferably

fit 1 suit, adapt, adjust; 2 proper, right,
suitable, qualified *improper*; 3 strong,
healthy, well *unfit*; 4 attack, seizure, spell,
spasm, convulsion, frenzy, rage

fitful irregular, sporadic, choppy, disconnected,
broken *regular, constant*

fix 1 mend, repair, adjust, regulate, doctor
break, impair; 2 settle, establish, stabilize,
solidify; 3 dilemma, quandary

fixture appliance, attachment, accessory

flag 1 signal, wave; 2 weaken, droop, wilt,
fade; 3 pennant, banner, standard, colours

flair talent, perception, insight

flamboyant flaming, brilliant, striking, ornate,
vivid, dazzling, fancy *simple*

flat 1 level, even, horizontal, smooth *uneven*;
2 dull, lifeless *exciting*; 3 off-key,
unmusical; 4 apartment, suite

flatter praise, compliment

flaunt display, exhibit, parade *hide, conceal*

flavour season, spice, give taste

flaw damage, defect, crack, fault, weakness,
blemish *perfection*

flay peel, skin, strip

fleck spot, mark, speckle, dot

flee run away, disappear

fleece 1 rob, cheat, swindle; 2 wool

fleet 1 rapid, swift, fast, quick, nimble *slow*;
2 ships; 3 group, band, company

flesh 1 meat, body; 2 skin; 3 family

flex bend, arch, curve *stiffen, straighten*

flimsy slight, frail, weak, delicate, dainty,
fragile *strong, sturdy*

flinch shrink, cringe, recoil, draw back

fling 1 throw, sling, pitch, toss, cast, hurl;
2 celebration, spree, escapade, lark

flippant rude, disrespectful, saucy, pert,
impudent, cocky, flip, cheeky, smart,
smart-alecky *polite*

float 1 buoy up, sustain, hold up *sink*;
2 raft; 3 parade car

flock group, crowd, throng, mob, bunch, pack,
multitude

flood overfill, drench, overflow, inundate,
oversupply, deluge

floor 1 defeat, overcome, upset, overthrow;
2 ground, pavement; 3 level, storey

flop 1 drop, fall, sink, go down, droop, slump,
sag *rise*; 2 fail, lose *succeed*

flounder 1 struggle, have trouble, stumble;
2 fish

flourish 1 thrive, prosper, grow, develop,
sprout, bloom *fade*; 2 wave, flaunt, display,
parade, exhibit, show

flout sneer, insult, mock, ridicule, jeer, taunt

flow glide, stream, pour, run, gush

flower blossom, bloom, develop, flourish, thrive

fluffy soft, downy, feathery, woolly, furry

fluid liquid, flowing, watery *solid*

flurry 1 fluster, excite, agitate, confuse, ruffle;
2 commotion, confusion, disturbance; 3 light
snowstorm

flush 1 blush, redden, colour; 2 rush, chase;
3 level, flat, even; 4 full, stuffed, packed

fluster excite, confuse

fly 1 glide, coast, sail, wing; 2 flee, run away;
3 insect

foam bubble, lather, froth

focus adjust, concentrate, make converge

foil 1 outwit, frustrate, thwart, spoil, ruin;
2 metal; 3 sword

fold 1 bend, double over *unfold*; 2 pen,
enclosure; 3 church

folk 1 people, persons, society, public; 2 tribe,
nation, race, clan, breed

follow 1 come next, succeed, ensue, trail *lead*,
precede; 2 pursue, trace; 3 use, obey, act
according to *ignore*

fond loving, liking, affectionate, adoring, romantic, sentimental, tender *disliking*

food edibles, provisions, nutriment, nourishment

fool 1 play, joke; 2 deceive, trick, mislead; 3 ninny, ignoramous, know-nothing, dunce, blockhead, scatterbrain, simpleton

foolhardy bold, rash, daring, audacious, reckless *cautious*

foolproof safe, tight, resistant

foot 1 walk, hoof it, march, hike; 2 part of body, sole; 3 base, lowest part, foundation *top*

footing 1 support, toehold, standing; 2 relationship, position

forage 1 hunt, search, look, explore; 2 animal food, fodder, feed, grain

forbear refrain, hold back, abstain, avoid, control oneself *indulge*

forbid prohibit, disallow, bar, ban, taboo, prevent, deter *encourage*

force 1 compel, make, drive, oblige, pressure, motivate; 2 thrust, push, shove, ram, break through; 3 power, strength, might, vigour, energy *weakness*; 4 group, body, staff, personnel, crew, gang

fore front, forward, foremost, first, chief, head, primary

foreboding warning, prediction, foretelling, forecast, promise, omen, prophecy, premonition

forecast prophecy, prediction, foretelling, promise, omen

foreign alien, external

foreman supervisor, superintendent, overseer, boss

foresee anticipate, predict, forecast, foretell, prophesy

foretell   predict, prophesy, forecast, promise
forever   always, evermore, eternity
forfeit   lose, sacrifice, let slip   *retain*
forge   1 make, shape, form, create, mould;
   2 counterfeit, falsify, make up;   3 progress,
   push onward;   4 blacksmith's shop, smelter
forget   not remember, escape one, lose sight of
   remember
forgive   pardon, excuse, absolve, quit   *blame*
forgo   give up, sacrifice, surrender, yield,
   relinquish, do without, waive   *retain, keep*
forlorn   hopeless, miserable, desperate,
   despondent, forsaken, abandoned, deserted,
   defenseless, helpless
form   1 develop, compose, make, create, fashion,
   construct, shape, mould;   2 kind, grade, type,
   variety, species, make;   3 manner, method,
   fashion, style, way, procedure
formal   orderly, regular, systematic,
   businesslike, stiff, arranged, structural,
   correct, proper, customary   *informal*
former   earlier, past, previous, preceding, prior,
   first   *latter*
formidable   difficult, hard, rough, rugged,
   tough   *easy, simple*
formulate   define, describe, express, voice, put
forsake   leave, give up, abandon, quit
forthcoming   approaching, imminent, coming,
   near, close
forthwith   immediately, promptly, without
   delay, instantly, at once, quickly, swiftly
fortify   strengthen, brace, invigorate,
   reinforce   *weaken*
fortitude   courage, strength, vigour, vitality,
   stamina, spunk   *weakness*
fortunate   lucky, auspicious   *unlucky*
fortune   1 riches, wealth, prosperity, treasure
   poverty;   2 luck, chance, fate, lot, destiny

forum 1 square, plaza; 2 discussion, debate, deliberation, consideration, study; 3 tribunal, law court

forward 1 send, dispatch, deliver, pass; 2 onward, ahead, frontward, advanced *backward*; 3 pert, bold, aggressive, insolent, presumptuous, brazen, immodest *shy*

fossil remains, trace, vestige, relic

foster nourish, nurture, feed, cultivate, nurse, care for, support, mind, tend, rear

foul 1 dirty, nasty, smelly, stinking, offensive, disgusting, vile *savoury*; 2 wicked, vicious, evil, bad, wrong, sinful, base, low *good*; 3 unfair *fair*

foundation 1 base, ground; 2 establishment, institution, organization

founder 1 fall, stumble, tumble, topple; 2 break down, collapse, sink, fail; 3 producer, creator, maker, author, originator, inventor, builder

foundry forge, smelter, blacksmith's shop

fowl bird, poultry

foxy crafty, shrewd, artful, cunning, knowing, sly, clever, canny *artless*

fraction part, portion, division, segment, section *whole*

fracture break, crack, burst, rupture, chip

fragile delicate, frail, slight, dainty, breakable, flimsy, brittle *sturdy, strong*

fragment part, portion, segment, section, fraction, division *whole*

fragrant sweet-smelling, perfumed, odorous, aromatic *foul*

frail weak, slight, delicate, dainty, fragile *strong*

frame 1 make, plan, put together, build, construct, form, design, devise, arrange; 2 border, edge, bound, trim; 3 body, figure, form; 4 support, skeleton

frank open, candid, sincere, straightforward, forthright, outspoken, blunt *deceitful*

frantic excited, frenzied, wild, violent, delirious, hysterical *calm, unexcited*

fraternal brotherly, kind, sympathetic, friendly, congenial, sociable *unfriendly, antisocial*

fraud cheating, trickery, dishonesty, swindle

fray 1 wear away, rub, tatter; 2 fight, quarrel, battle, conflict, clash, brush, tussle, skirmish, scuffle, struggle, melee

free 1 clear, acquit, dismiss, release, discharge, relieve, reprieve, deliver, liberate, emancipate *enslave*; 2 loose, unfastened, untied *restrained*; 3 independent, open, unrestrained, at liberty *restricted*; 4 complimentary, gratis, untaxed, without charge *taxed*

freeze 1 chill, refrigerate *thaw, defrost*; 2 stiffen, remain motionless

freight load, cargo, burden, shipment, goods

frenzy fury, madness, excitement, passion, rage, agitation, fit, delirium *serenity, calmness*

frequent 1 visit often, haunt; 2 many, recurrent, common, prevalent, regular, habitual *infrequent*

fresh 1 new, unused, firsthand, original *old, stale*; 2 unsalty; 3 bright, alert, unfaded, brisk, vigorous, energetic, refreshed *dull*

friction resistance, clash, conflict, grinding, scraping *harmony*

friend acquaintance, intimate, companion, comrade, mate, associate, colleague, partner, crony, playmate, chum *enemy*

fright 1 fear, terror, alarm, dismay, dread, awe, horror, phobia, panic *fearlessness*; 2 eyesore, mess *beauty*

frigid 1 cold, stiff, chilling, icy, reserved, unfeeling, restrained, aloof, distant *warm, friendly*; 2 freezing, wintry, crisp, brisk, nippy, raw, sharp, frosty *warm*

frivolous silly, shallow, unimportant, light, trivial, foolish, inane *serious, important*

front fore, first part, face, head *back*

frontier border, edge

frost freezing, cold

froth 1 foam, lather; 2 trivia, rubbish, unimportant *important*

frown scowl, pout, look sullen, look displeased *smile*

frugal economical, thrifty, saving, prudent *wasteful*

frustrate foil, thwart, defeat, spoil, ruin *aid, help*

fuel kindling, combustible

fugitive 1 runaway, escaping; 2 temporary, passing, transient *lasting, permanent*

fulfil perform, do, carry out, execute, finish, complete, transact, discharge, satisfy

full 1 complete, entire, stuffed, packed, crammed *empty*; 2 plump, round, fat *thin*; 3 broad, wide, expansive, roomy *skimpy*

fume 1 be angry, burn, seethe, rage, storm, rave; 2 smoke, vapour, gas

fumigate disinfect, sterilize

fun amusement, playfulness, joking, sport, good time, pleasure, entertainment, enjoyment

function 1 work, be used, act, operate, perform, serve; 2 ceremony, gathering, service, rite, ritual, exercise

fund stock, supply, resources, assets

fundamental essential, basic, underlying, primary, elementary

funeral   burial, last rites
furious   raging, violent, angry, mad, rabid,
overwrought, upset, enraged, infuriated
calm, placid
furnace   stove, heater, oven, kiln, forge
furnish   supply, provide, give, equip, outfit
furrow   wrinkle, crease, groove
further   1 help, aid, advance, promote
hinder;   2 farther, beyond, past, over
furthermore   in addition, then, again, also,
too, besides, similarly, likewise, by the same
token
furtive   secret, sly, stealthy, sneaky,
underhand   *open, honest*
fuse   1 join, blend, melt, unite, combine, stick
together, weld, solder, glue   *separate*;
2 exploder, blaster
fuss   worry, bother, fret
futile   useless, vain, unsuccessful, ineffective
useful
future   coming, hereafter, tomorrow   *past*

G

gadget   device, tool, instrument, implement,
utensil, apparatus, appliance, contraption
gag   1 silence, muzzle, muffle, stop one's mouth,
restrain;   2 joke, jest
gain   1 get, obtain, secure, acquire, earn,
receive   *lose*;   2 benefit;   3 advance, make
progress, improve, look up, pick up, come
along   *deteriorate*
gala   festive, merry, gay, jolly, joyous, joyful
gale   1 wind, windstorm, tempest, squall;
2 noisy outburst, shout
gallant   1 brave, courageous, valiant, bold,
heroic   *cowardly*;   2 noble, chivalrous,
courteous, knightly, manly, fine, grand,
stately   *ungentlemanly, ill-mannered*

gallery 1 passage, corridor, hallway, arcade;
2 balcony, grandstand
gallows hanging, execution, rope, noose
gamble speculate, risk, bet, wager, try one's
luck
game 1 brave, plucky, spirited, daring
unwilling; 2 contest, match, play, fun;
3 scheme, plan, plot; 4 hunted animals,
wildlife, quarry, prey
gang group, crew, ring, band, party, company,
pack, troop, bunch, crowd
gangway passageway, bridge
gap 1 break, opening, pass, cleft, crevice, rift,
gulf, hole; 2 blank, unfilled space
gape 1 yawn, open mouth wide; 2 gap, gulf
hole, opening
garbage waste, scraps, refuse, rubbish, trash,
debris, litter, junk
gargle mouthwash, antiseptic
garland wreath, spray, bouquet
garnish decorate, trim, adorn, beautify,
embellish, dress up, spruce up, fix up
garrison 1 fort, stronghold; 2 military unit,
regiment, battalion, company, troop
gas vapour, fume
gash cut, wound, laceration
gasp pant, puff, choke
gather 1 collect, bring together, assemble,
accumulate, amass, bunch, group, cluster,
compile *scatter*; 2 fold, tuck, pleat
gaudy showy, tasteless, garish, vulgar
tasteful
gauge measure, estimate, judge, rate, apraise,
assess, size up
gaunt 1 thin, lean, skinny, scrawny, lanky,
bony; 2 desolate, blank, bleak, empty
gay 1 happy, merry, spirited, lively, animated,
vivacious, playful, joyful, joyous, jolly, jovial,

cheerful, pleasant *unhappy, solemn*;
2 colourful, bright, vivid, rich *dull*

gaze stare, gape, gawk

general 1 common, widespread, indefinite,
vague, broad; 2 officer, commander

generate produce, cause, bring about, create,
originate

generous 1 unselfish, giving, kind, liberal,
openhanded, bighearted *selfish*; 2 large,
plentiful, ample *small*

genial pleasant, cheerful, friendly, kindly,
warm, comforting, cordial, agreeable,
amiable, good-natured *disagreeable,
unpleasant*

genius 1 intelligence, inspiration, talent,
creative thought, gift; 2 prodigy, master,
wizard

genocide slaughter, massacre, killing,
butchery, carnage

gentle 1 mild, soft, moderate, tender *rough*;
2 kindly, friendly, good-natured, cordial,
genial, amiable, sympathetic, humane
harsh, mean; 3 refined, well-bred, cultured,
polished, genteel, noble *ill-bred*

genuine real, true, authentic, pure, legitimate,
bona fide, sincere *fake*

germ 1 seed, origin, beginning; 2 micro-
organism

germinate grow, develop, sprout, flourish,
thrive

gesture signal, sign, motion, movement

get 1 obtain, receive, gain, fetch, bring,
retrieve, acquire, secure *give*; 2 become,
turn, grow; 3 persuade, influence, induce;
4 incur, bring about

geyser spring, steam, volcanic water, jet, gush,
fountain

ghastly 1 horrible, terrible, dreadful, deplorable, outrageous, vile, wretched, detestable, contemptible, frightful, shocking, appalling, repulsive *lovely, beautiful*; 2 pale, sallow, deathlike *ruddy*

ghost spirit, spectre, phantom, spook

giant huge, immense, vast, enormous, tremendous, colossal, monumental, mammoth, gigantic *tiny, minute*

gift 1 present, offering; 2 ability, talent, endowment, power, aptitude

gigantic huge, immense, vast, enormous, tremendous, colossal, monumental, mammoth *tiny, minute*

giggle laugh, chuckle, titter, snicker

gild 1 coat, paint, cover; 2 sweeten, embellish

girth size, dimensions, measure, proportions, width, expanse

give 1 present, offer, hand over, bestow, donate, contribute, grant, award, furnish, provide, supply, allot, deliver, deal out, dole out, mete out *take*; 2 yield, bend

given 1 presented, handed over; 2 stated, supposed, assumed; 3 inclined, disposed, addicted, bent

glacier icefield

glad happy, pleased, bright, gay, delighted, charmed, thrilled, tickled, gratified, satisfied, joyful, joyous, cheerful *sad*

glade clearing, open space

gladiator fighter, battler, combatant, contestant, contender, competitor

glamorous fascinating, charming, entrancing, enchanting, bewitching, spellbinding, alluring, captivating, enthralling, attractive, interesting, appealing, enticing *unattractive*

glare 1 stare, scowl, glower; 2 shine, glow, burn, glaze, flash, flare, dazzle, blind

glaze gloss, polish, lustre, buff, wax, coat, cover

gleam shine, glow, beam, glare, radiate, burn, glimmer, glisten, twinkle, sparkle

glean gather, harvest, reap, pick, separate, select

glee joy, delight, mirth, happiness, gladness, cheer, enchantment, elation, bliss, merriment *sadness*

glide cruise, coast, skim, slide, sweep, flow, sail, fly, move easily

glimmer 1 shimmer, blink, flicker; 2 hint, indication, suggestion, inkling, clue

glimpse glance, see, notice, catch sight of

glisten sparkle, glitter, shine, glimmer, twinkle

glitter sparkle, glimmer, twinkle, shine, glisten

gloat exult, triumph, glory

globe 1 sphere, ball; 2 earth, world, universe; 3 map

gloomy 1 dark, dim, dismal, dreary, sombre, bleak, depressing, discouraging; 2 sad, melancholy, glum *cheerful*

glorify worship, praise, laud, exalt, extol, honour, ennoble *belittle*

glorious magnificent, splendid, grand, superb, fine, impressive, proud, stately, majestic, elegant, luxurious, extravagant *terrible*

gloss shine, lustre, sheen, glow, gleam

glossary wordlist, dictionary, wordbook, thesaurus

glow 1 burn, blaze, flame, flare, flicker, shine, radiate, glare, dazzle; 2 redden, blush, flush; 3 tingle, tremble, shiver, quiver, quake, thrill

glower stare, scowl, glare, frown

glum sad, gloomy, dismal, sullen, moody *cheerful*

glutton greedy eater

gnarled knotted, twisted, rugged

gnash crunch, gnaw, grind

go 1 move, leave, travel, pass, proceed, advance *come*; 2 act, work; 3 become, get to be, turn, grow into; 4 operate, function; 5 be given, aim, point, head for; 6 belong, have place

goad urge, drive, push, shove, poke, jab, spur

goal 1 end, finish, destination, objective, aim, object, target; 2 score, point

gobble 1 eat fast, devour, gulp, gorge, stuff; 2 turkey talk

goblet glass, cup, drinking vessel, beaker

goblin spirit, elf, troll, dwarf

good 1 excellent, fine, nice, splendid; 2 well-behaved, proper *bad*; 3 desirable, right, appropriate, fitting, suitable, becoming, satisfying, seemly, nice, decent *undesirable*; 4 kind, friendly, gracious, nice, warmhearted, sympathetic, brotherly, fraternal *unkind, unfriendly*; 5 real, genuine, authentic, legitimate, bona fide *fake*; 6 benefit, profit, advantage

good-bye farewell, so long, adieu *hello*

goods 1 belongings, property, holdings, possessions; 2 wares, merchandise

good will willingness, agreeability, readiness, friendly relations, harmony

gorge 1 stuff, devour, gulp, gobble; 2 valley, ravine, gully

gorgeous splendid, beautiful, ravishing, stunning, glorious, divine, brilliant, dazzling *hideous*

gory bloody

gossip chat, talk, tattle, prattle, rumour, hearsay

gouge dig, scoop, excavate, burrow, chisel, carve

govern rule, control, manage, regulate, influence, determine, head, lead, command, preside over, direct, supervise, minister, guide, conduct, handle, run, boss

grab snatch, seize, grasp, grip, clutch

grace 1 honour, dignify, distinguish, *dishonour*; 2 beauty, loveliness, attractiveness; 3 charm, elegance, taste, refinement, polish, culture *tactlessness, vulgarity*; 4 sympathy, clemency, mercy, pardon, excuse, reprieve; 5 favour; 6 thanks, prayer, thanksgiving, blessing

gracious pleasant, kindly, courteous, good, nice, warmhearted, sympathetic, polite, respectful, cordial, friendly, hospitable, generous *rude, unkind*

grade 1 arrange, sort, classify, group, rank, rate, mark, place; 2 slope, incline, hill

gradual slow, little by little, easy *sudden*

graduate finish, pass, succeed, advance *fail*

graft 1 transplant, join; 2 bribery, corruption; 3 work

grain 1 particle, speck, bit; 2 plant, seed; 3 texture, finish, markings, fibre; 4 character, temper, nature, disposition, tendency

grand 1 large, great, considerable, sizable, big *small*; 2 important, main, outstanding, prominent, distinguished, magnificent, glorious, impressive, majestic, dignified, stately *unimportant, insignificant*

grant 1 give, donate, present, bestow, award, allot, give out, deal out, mete out, dole out; 2 allow, permit, let, consent, admit *deny*

graph diagram, chart, plot, outline, draw up

graphic lifelike, vivid, meaningful, significant, representative, descriptive, pictorial

grapple 1 seize, grip, grab, grasp, clutch, clasp, hold *release*; 2 struggle, fight

grasp 1 seize, hold, grapple, clutch, grip;
2 control, possession, hold, command,
domination; 3 understanding,
comprehension

grate 1 grind, file, scrape, pulverize; 2 scrape,
scratch, rasp; 3 annoy, irritate, get on one's
nerves, rub the wrong way; 4 iron bars,
grillwork

grateful thankful, appreciative, obliged
ungrateful

gratify satisfy, please

gratitude thankfulness, gratefulness,
appreciation *ungratefulness*

grave 1 serious, solemn, grim, earnest,
thoughtful, sober, sombre *cheerful, gay*;
2 dignified, slow-moving, stately, imposing,
majestic; 3 important, vital, essential
unimportant; 4 burial place, plot

gravitate move toward, incline, lean, tend

graze 1 feed; 2 touch lightly, scrape, rub,
contact, brush, skim

grease oil, lubrication, fat

great 1 large, grand, sizable, considerable
small; 2 outstanding, prominent, famous,
main, distinguished, remarkable, glorious,
magnificent, impressive, majestic, stately
insignificant, unimportant

greed avarice, piggishness, hoggishness, lust,
desire

green 1 undeveloped, unripe, immature *ripe*;
2 untrained, new, inexperienced, ignorant
experienced

grieve hurt, mourn, brood over, lament, sorrow

grievance wrong, evil, protest, objection,
injury, injustice, complaint

grill 1 broil, cook, barbecue; 2 question, cross-
examine, interrogate; 3 gridiron, grating

grim 1 stern, strict, harsh, fierce, merciless, rough, unyielding, rigid, inflexible, adamant *relaxed, lenient*; 2 horrible, frightful, ghastly, dreadful, terrible *pleasant*

grimace wry face

grime dirt, soot, smut, mud, slime, filth

grin smile, smirk, beam

grind 1 crush, pulverize, grate, crumble, mash, squash; 2 sharpen, smooth, rub, edge, whet, file; 3 study, work, drudge, plod

grip 1 seize, hold, grasp, clutch, clasp, clench *release*; 2 suitcase, handbag, valise; 3 control, command, domination, possession; 4 understanding, comprehension

grit 1 grind, rub, grate; 2 gravel, sand, grain; 3 courage, pluck, stamina

groan moan, harsh sound, wail, howl

groove 1 channel, furrow, track, rut; 2 routine

grope feel around, fumble, poke around

gross 1 whole, entire, total; 2 bad, terrible, stupid; 3 coarse, vulgar, unrefined, crude *refined*; 4 big, fat, obese, bulky, massive, clumsy *petite, delicate*; 5 thick, heavy, dense *slight*

grotesque 1 fantastic, incredible, bizarre, monstrous, ridiculous, absurd; 2 deformed, unnatural, queer, odd, disfigured, ill-shaped, ugly *natural, normal*

grouch complain, grumble, mutter, mope, sulk, fret

ground 1 fix, establish, root, set; 2 surface, soil, sod, dirt, land, base, floor

grounds 1 lawns, garden, real estate; 2 dregs, leftovers, sediment; 3 foundation, basis, reason, cause, premise, motive

group arrange, assemble, cluster, organize, grade, sort, classify, gather, collect, bunch *disassemble*

grovel crawl, creep, cower

grow 1 increase, mature, become, advance, gain, rise, develop, age, progress *shrink, decrease*; 2 raise, farm, cultivate

growl snarl, complain, grumble

grub 1 dig, gouge, excavate, scoop out, tunnel, burrow; 2 toil, drudge, plod; 3 larva; 4 food

grudge ill will, dislike

grudgingly unwillingly, reluctantly, involuntarily, under protest, against one's will *willingly*

grumble complain, mutter

guarantee promise, secure, pledge, swear, warrant, assure, certify, sponsor, back, endorse, underwrite, stand for

guard 1 watch, defend, shield, protect, secure; 2 check, restrain, control, curb

guess think, believe, suppose, assume, imagine, consider, conjecture

guest visitor, caller, company *host*

guide 1 lead, direct, show, steer, escort, conduct, squire, usher; 2 manage, control, regulate, advise, instruct, govern, rule

guild society, union

guile deceit, cunning, craftiness, sneakiness

guilty criminal, to blame, at fault, blameworthy, culpable

guise 1 garb, dress, cover, coat, attire, clothes, apparel; 2 appearance, look, show, form, manner

gulch valley, gorge, ravine, gully, canyon

gulf 1 separation, break, cut, cleft, crack, crevice, hole, rift, opening, gap, chasm, pit; 2 bay

gullible easily fooled, naive, deceivable

gully gorge, valley, ditch, ravine, gulf, gulch

gush 1 rush out, pour, flow, spout, surge, flush, flood, spurt; 2 chatter, babble, prattle

gutter   channel, groove, trench, ditch
gymnasium   arena, athletic field, playground, court
gymnastics   exercises, drill, athletics, calisthenics, sports, acrobatics

H

habit   1 custom, practice, nature, pattern, trait;   2 religious dress
habitation   abode, dwelling place, residence, lodging, housing
hack   1 cut, sever, split, cleave, chop;   2 cough
hag   witch, crone
haggard   thin, poor, pale, deathlike, wild-eyed, tired-looking, seedy
hall   1 passageway, corridor, arcade, vestibule, lobby, foyer;   2 large meeting room, assembly, auditorium;   3 building, community centre, theatre
halt   stop, come to a standstill, check, arrest, quit, cease, end
halve   divide, dissect, split, share
hamper   1 hinder, impede, cramp, obstruct, block, restrain, limit   *help*;   2 basket
hand   1 give, turn over, deliver, transfer, pass;   2 worker, person, labourer;   3 possession, central power, command, grasp, clutches;   4 handwriting, penmanship
handicap   hindrance, burden, disadvantage, load   *asset*
handle   1 touch, feel, finger, manipulate, use;   2 manage, direct, regulate, carry on, govern, run;   3 deal in, trade in
handsome   1 good-looking, attractive   *ugly*;   2 large, considerable, big, generous, liberal   *meagre*
handy   1 useful, convenient, nearby, available, ready   *inconvenient*;   2 skilful, adept, apt, proficient   *inept*

hang 1 suspend, fasten up; 2 execute, string up; 3 droop, bend down, sag

haphazard chance, random, casual *planned*

happen 1 take place, occur, come off, pass; 2 chance, turn up

happy contented, glad, joyful, blissful, cheerful, bright, radiant *unhappy, sad*

harass 1 trouble, torment, molest, bother, badger, plague, persecute, haunt, bully, threaten; 2 disturb, worry, vex

harbour 1 shelter, protect, shield, defend, guard, screen, cover, house; 2 keep in mind, consider, think, entertain the idea; 3 port, dock, wharf, pier

hard 1 firm, solid, stony, rigid *soft*; 2 stern, unyielding, strict, inflexible *easygoing*; 3 difficult, rough, rugged, tough *easy*; 4 with effort, with vigour, laboriously, strenuously; 5 unpleasant, harsh, ugly, severe, callous *pleasant*

hardly barely, just, not quite, scarcely, narrowly, nearly

hardship trouble, ups and downs

hardy 1 strong, healthy, robust, mighty, powerful, sturdy, rugged, hale *weak*; 2 bold, daring, courageous, valiant, gallant, heroic *cowardly*

harm hurt, damage, wrong, injure, impair *help, improve*

harmonious 1 agreeing, in accord, congenial, compatible *conflicting*; 2 musical, in tune, blending

harness 1 control, use; 2 saddle, hitch up, yoke, hook up

harsh 1 rough, coarse, husky, grating, raspy, gruff *smooth*; 2 cruel, unfeeling, severe, bitter, sharp, cutting, piercing, gruff, brusque, curt, strict, stern, tough *kind*

harvest 1 reap, gather, pick; 2 crop, yield, product, proceeds; 3 result, consequences, effect, outcome

hasty 1 quick, hurried, fast, swift, speedy, rapid, fleet *slow*; 2 rash, reckless, unprepared, sudden, premature, impulsive, impetuous *planned*; 3 quick-tempered, hotheaded

hatch 1 arrange, plan, plot, scheme, intrigue, invent, concoct, make up; 2 produce, generate, incubate, breed, brood, be born; 3 opening, door, trap

hate dislike, loathe, detest, abhor, abominate *love*

haughty arrogant, proud, lofty, scornful *modest*

haul 1 pull, drag, draw, heave, tug, tow; 2 take, catch

haunt 1 visit often, frequent, hang around; 2 obsess, torment

have 1 hold, possess, own; 2 must, be forced, should, ought, need; 3 cause, make, compel, require; 4 experience, feel, meet, undergo, endure; 5 permit, tolerate, suffer, put up with, stand for

haven shelter, safety, harbour, refuge, sanctuary

havoc destruction, ruin, devastation, ravage, damage, harm, injury *restoration*

hawk 1 hunt, chase; 2 peddle, sell, vend; 3 falcon, kestrel

hazard risk, chance, gamble, bet, wager

hazy 1 misty, smoky, dim, cloudy, overcast, foggy; 2 obscure, indistinct, unclear, indefinite, vague, faint, blurred, fuzzy, uncertain, confused, muddled *clear*

head 1 lead, come first, precede, initiate *follow*; 2 govern, command, lead, direct,

manage, supervise, administer, control, rule,
dominate, conduct, run; 3 proceed, move
toward, go, gravitate; 4 pate, crown, top;
5 mind, intelligence, understanding,
mentality, brain; 6 crisis, conclusion

headfirst hastily, rashly, impetuously,
impulsively, recklessly, carelessly
cautiously

heading topic, title, subject, issue, question,
theme, headline

headquarters main office, base, central station

headstrong obstinate, stubborn, wilful,
bullheaded

headway progress, advance, improvement
setback

heal cure, remedy, correct, mend, repair
damage, impair

health well-being, physical condition *sickness*

heap pile, gather, fill, stack, load

hear listen, heed

heart 1 body pump; 2 feelings, soul, spirit,
temperament; 3 kindness, sympathy,
warmth, love, affection; 4 courage,
enthusiasm, stamina *cowardice*; 5 middle,
centre, core, nucleus, hub; 6 substance,
main part, meat

hearten cheer, encourage, inspire, gladden
dishearten

heartfelt sincere, genuine, profound, deep
insecure

heartily sincerely, warmly, devotedly,
completely, fervently, ardently *indifferently*

heat 1 warm, make hot *cool*; 2 cook,
prepare; 3 excite, move, affect, stir, provoke,
arouse, kindle, inflame *calm*

heave 1 lift, raise, hoist, pull, haul, lug, tug,
tow, drag; 2 breathe hard, pant; 3 swell,
rise, bulge, billow, surge *subside*

heaven 1 sky, space; 2 paradise, bliss, ecstasy *hell*

heavy weighted, laden, bulky, fat, hefty *light, thin*

hectic 1 feverish, heated, hot, burning; 2 exciting, stirring, frantic, moving, busy *calm*

hedge 1 dodge, sidestep, evade questions, duck; 2 boundary, limit, border, borderline

heed notice, observe, follow, care, mind, attend *ignore*

height 1 altitude, elevation, tallness, stature; 2 top, summit, highest point, peak, crown, tip, apex, acme *bottom*

help 1 aid, assist, lend a hand, avail *hinder*; 2 benefit, relieve; 3 avoid, prevent, deter, keep from

hem border, edge, rim

hence 1 therefore, consequently, accordingly, because of this, thus; 2 away, elsewhere; 3 later, from now, in future time

herald 1 announce, bring news, proclaim, cry out, shout; 2 messenger

herd flock, assemble, join together, drive, shepherd, collect, gather *scatter*

here 1 this place, this spot *there*; 2 now, at present, at this time *later*; 3 present, in attendance *absent*

hereditary inherited, inborn

heresy misbelief, dissent

heritage heredity, birthright

hermit recluse, stay-at-home

heroic brave, gallant, valiant, stalwart, courageous, bold, chivalrous *cowardly*

hesitate 1 pause, rest, let up; 2 feel doubtful, be undecided, flounder, falter, waver

hibernate sleep, slumber, hole up for winter

hide 1 conceal, cover up, screen, cloak, veil, mask *expose*; 2 skin, pelt

hideous ugly, frightful, horrible, horrid,
dreadful, terrible, repulsive, ghastly
beautiful

high 1 tall, long, lofty, elevated, steep,
towering, soaring; 2 great, chief, main,
important, eminent, exalted, grand
unimportant; 3 shrill, sharp, piercing,
screechy *low*

high-strung sensitive, nervous, excitable,
edgy, jumpy *calm, steady*

highway road, thoroughfare, turnpike,
motorway

hilarious merry, gay, joyful, gleeful

hinder stop, obstruct, impede, check, curb,
retard, restrain, hold back *help*

hinge 1 fasten, clasp, lock *separate*;
2 depend, rest on, revolve on

hint suggest, imply, intimate, insinuate

hire 1 employ, engage *fire*; 2 lease, let, rent,
charter

history record, chronicle, annals

hit 1 strike, blow, knock, punch, poke, smack,
whack, slug, bat, crack, swat, sock, clout;
2 meet, find, discover, come upon, reach,
arrive at *miss*; 3 affect, impress, strike;
4 success *failure*

hitch 1 fasten, hook, clasp, bind, tie
separate; 2 jerk, yank; 3 obstacle, stopping,
block, catch, snag, difficulty, drawback

hoard save, store, collect, accumulate, amass,
gather *use*

hoarse rough, gruff, harsh, husky

hobby avocation, pastime

hoe plough, dig, loosen, till

hoist raise, lift, elevate, boost *lower*

hold 1 grasp, keep, grip, cling to, clutch,
retain *release*; 2 contain, support, bear,
carry; 3 have, maintain, occupy; 4 apply,

be true, stand up;   5 think, consider,
suppose, assume, presume, regard, surmise

holding   land, property, possession, ownership,
title, claim, stake

hole   opening, hollow, pit, gap, chasm, cavity

holiday   vacation, leave, furlough, festival

hollow   1 empty, vacant, bare, void, blank,
barren *occupied*;   2 deep, sunken, concave
bulging;   3 false, unreal, insincere
sincere;   4 hungry, starved, famished,
ravenous, empty *full*

holy   sacred, spiritual, pure, religious, godly

homage   respect, honour, reverence, regard,
esteem, deference, acknowledgment
disrespect

home   1 abode, dwelling, residence, hearth,
habitat;   2 institution, sanitorium, hospital,
asylum

homeland   native land, mother country

homely   1 ugly, plain, unattractive;   2 simple,
ordinary, common;   3 homelike, comfortable,
cozy, domestic

homestead   farm, plantation, house and
grounds

homework   lesson, task, assignment, exercise,
duty

honest   fair, upright, truthful, frank, open,
genuine, pure, sincere *dishonest, insincere*

honour   glory, fame, renown, respect, regard,
esteem, homage, deference, praise *dishonour*

hook   1 fasten, clasp, bind, clip, snap, latch
unhook;   2 catch, snare, trap *release*;
3 hanger, wire, crook

hop   spring, jump, vault

hope   wish for, desire, yearn for, expect

horizontal   level, flat, even, plane

horrible   frightful, shocking, terrible, dreadful,
outrageous, horrid, ghastly, deplorable,
scandalous *splendid*

hospitable friendly, receptive, welcoming, cordial, amiable, gracious, neighbourly, generous *unfriendly*

hospital clinic, sanatorium

host 1 receptionist, proprietor; 2 large number, quantity, multitude, score, flock, army, swarm

hostel inn, hotel, tavern, roadhouse

hostile unfriendly, unfavourable, bitter, antagonistic, aggressive, belligerent, militant *friendly*

hot 1 torrid, burning, boiling, fiery *cold*; 2 spicy, sharp, peppery, nippy, tangy *bland*; 3 fresh, new *stale*

hotel inn, tavern, roadhouse, lodging, hostel, motel

hothouse greenhouse, nursery, conservatory

hound 1 hunt, chase, seek, search, follow; 2 urge, press, insist; 3 dog

house 1 shelter, building, dwelling, lodge, residence, home; 2 audience, congregation

hover 1 float, sail, drift; 2 waver, hesitate, pause, falter

however 1 nevertheless, although, notwithstanding, yet, still, but; 2 whatever, whatsoever

howl cry, yell, shout, bawl, scream, screech, roar, bellow, bark, yelp, wail

hub centre, middle, nucleus, core

hubbub noise, uproar, racket, din, clamour, tumult, commotion, ado, fuss, turmoil, bustle, row, rumpus *calm*

huddle assemble, crowd, gather, flock together, cluster, congregate *scatter*

huff 1 puff, blow, exhale; 2 fit of anger

hug hold, clasp, embrace, press, enfold, squeeze

huge great, very large, vast, immense, massive enormous, monumental, gigantic, tremendous *tiny*

hulk 1 ship, boat; 2 oaf, lout, clod

hum 1 drone, buzz, murmur; 2 active, busy *quiet, inactive*

humane kind, good, gracious, warmhearted, sympathetic *cruel*

humble modest, meek, plain, simple, homely, unpretentious *vain, showy*

humid moist, damp, wet, muggy *dry*

humiliate embarrass, disgrace, shame, mortify, offend, insult, dishonour *honour, dignify*

humour 1 cater to, give in to, pamper, spoil, coddle, oblige, please, satisfy; 2 wit, pleasantry, comedy; 3 mood, temper, frame of mind, disposition

hunch 1 hump, bump, bulge; 2 feeling, suspicion, impression

hunger desire, eagerness, appetite, craving

hunt search, seek, look, pursue, chase

hurdle 1 leap, jump, vault, bound; 2 obstacle, block, difficulty, hitch, catch, snag, barrier

hurl throw, fling, sling, pitch, toss, cast, heave, chuck, flip

hurricane storm, cyclone, blizzard, tornado, squall

hurry hasten, speed, urge, rush, accelerate, hustle

hurt injure, bruise, harm, damage, wrong, impair, pain, wound, distress, grieve, offend *help, benefit, soothe*

husband 1 save, economize, preserve, keep, reserve, scrimp, skimp; 2 spouse, mate, married man

hush silence, quiet, mute, muffle, calm

husky 1 strong, sturdy, mighty, powerful, rugged, strapping, well-built, muscular, athletic, hefty, beefy; 2 hoarse, harsh, rough, coarse, raspy *smooth*; 3 Eskimo dog

hustle 1 hasten, speed, urge, rush; 2 push, shove, jostle, prod, bump, jolt, bounce

hut cabin, shed, shanty, shack
hybrid mongrel, crossbreed, half-breed
hydrophobia rabies
hypnotize entrance, spellbind, mesmerize
hypocrite pretender
hysterical uncontrollable, frenzied, frantic,
  delirious, beside oneself, overexcited, upset
  calm, composed

I

icing frosting, topping
idea thought, plan, notion, fancy, opinion
ideal perfect, faultless, flawless, model *faulty,
  imperfect*
identical same, alike, exactly like, duplicate
  different
identify recognize, know, place, distinguish,
  make out, name, tell, label, tag, designate
idiot simpleton, imbecile, moron, half-wit, fool
idle 1 inactive, unoccupied, at leisure *busy*;
  2 lazy, loafing *ambitious*; 3 useless, vain,
  futile, worthless *worthwhile*;
  4 unwarranted, groundless, unfounded
idol god
ignite burn, set afire, light, kindle, stoke
ignorant unintelligent, foolish, uninformed,
  unaware, uneducated *smart, knowledgeable*
ignore disregard, overlook, snub, slight,
  avoid *mind, heed*
ill 1 sick, ailing, unwell, indisposed, out of
  sorts, below par, under the weather
  healthy; 2 evil, bad, wrong *good*
illegal unlawful, criminal, illegitimate *legal*
illegible unclear, indistinct, unreadable
  legible, clear
illiterate uneducated, uncultured, unlearned,
  ignorant *learned, educated*

illogical unreasonable, senseless, unsound, unscientific *logical*

illuminate 1 light, brighten, spotlight; 2 clarify, explain, simplify, show, illustrate

illusion deception, delusion, trick, misconception

illustrate 1 clarify, explain, show, demonstrate; 2 represent, picture, portray

illustrious famous, great, outstanding, splendid, radiant, bright, shining, glorious

image likeness, representation, picture, reflection, resemblance, vision, appearance

imagine 1 envisage, fancy, conceive, dream; 2 suppose, guess, assume, presume, gather

imitate copy, act like, repeat, mirror, reflect, echo, emulate

immaculate pure, clean, spotless *dirty*

immature undeveloped, unripe, inexperienced, green, childish *mature*

immediately instantly, at once, without delay, now, promptly, straightaway, forthwith, quickly, swiftly, directly *later*

immense huge, large, vast, great, stupendous, enormous, monumental, mammoth, gigantic, giant *tiny*

immerse 1 submerge, plunge, sink, dip, inundate, drown, dunk; 2 absorb, engross, occupy, engage, grip, hold, fascinate, enthrall

immigrate enter, come into *leave*

imminent forthcoming, approaching, nearing, impending, coming up

immoral wrong, wicked, evil, bad, sinful *moral*

immortal everlasting, undying, eternal

immovable fixed, firm, steadfast, stable, stationary *movable*

immune resistant, exempt, clear, excused, spared, let off *subject to*

impact collision, crash, bump, clash, shock, brunt

impair damage, harm, weaken, hurt, make worse, break *improve*

impartial fair, neutral, unprejudiced, unbiased, uninfluenced, indifferent *prejudiced*

impassioned emotional, ardent, passionate, fervent, earnest, sincere, serious, excited *indifferent*

impassive unmoved, unfeeling, unemotional, unresponsive, unsympathetic *emotional*

impatient restless, anxious, eager, intolerant *patient*

impede hinder, obstruct, curb, inhibit, arrest, check, interrupt, retard, delay, limit, confine, cramp, hamper *facilitate*

impel drive, force, cause, push, move, propel, stimulate, compel, make

impenetrable 1 unapproachable, inaccessible, impassable, dense *open, passable*; 2 obscure, unclear, vague, unintelligible *clear*

imperative urgent, necessary, compulsory, compelling, pressing, crucial, critical, mandatory *unnecessary*

imperceptible slight, vague, unclear *noticeable*

imperfect defective, faulty, incomplete, inadequate, deficient, impaired, blemished, marred *perfect*

imperial supreme, majestic, magnificent, regal, royal

impersonal impartial, neutral, unbiased, detached, unprejudiced *biased*

impertinence insolence, impudence, rudeness, brazenness, cockiness *respectfulness, courtesy*

impetuous hasty, rash, sudden, abrupt, impulsive, unexpected, reckless *restrained, careful, thoughtful*

impetus driving force, momentum, thrust, push

implement 1 carry out, get done, bring about, complete *neglect*; 2 tool, utensil, instrument, apparatus, device, appliance, contraption

implore beg, plead, appeal, entreat, beseech, pray

imply suggest, hint, intimate, infer, insinuate

import 1 bring in, receive, take in, admit, introduce *export*; 2 meaning, significance, implication, substance, effect, importance

important meaningful, valuable, influential, significant, substantial, prominent, outstanding *unimportant*

impose put, place, set, charge, levy, tax, burden with, force

imposing impressive, dramatic, spectacular, grand, magnificent, splendid, noble, glorious, proud, stately, majestic, elegant *unimpressive*

impossible inconceivable, unimaginable, absurd, unthinkable *possible*

imposter pretender, deceiver cheat, impersonator, fraud, faker

impoverish make poor, ruin, break, bankrupt, exhaust, deplete *enrich*

impractical unfeasible, unworkable, unrealistic *practical*

impregnable resistant, strong, unconquerable, unassailable, invincible *vulnerable*

impress 1 affect, strike; 2 fix, establish, root, plant, stamp; 3 mark, imprint, engrave

imprint mark, engrave, impress, stamp

imprison jail, confine, lock up *free, release*

improbable unlikely, doubtful, questionable *probable*

improper 1 wrong, incorrect, unsuitable,
  inappropriate, unfit, bad; 2 indecent,
  unbecoming *proper*
improve better, perfect, progress, mend,
  develop, advance *worsen*
improvise invent, make up, devise, originate,
  dream up, dash off, ad-lib
imprudent rash, indiscreet, overconfident,
  unwise, unsound, unreasonable,
  unintelligent, ill-advised *careful, prudent*
impudent forward, bold, immodest, pert,
  impertinent, rude, disrespectful, brash,
  saucy *polite, courteous*
impulse 1 thrust, push, urge, pressure,
  compulsion; 2 notion, sudden thought,
  fancy, flash, inspiration
impure 1 dirty, unclean, polluted,
  contaminated, infected *clean, pure*; 2 bad,
  corrupt, indecent, obscene, foul, filthy,
  nasty *clean, decent*
inability incapability, ineptitude,
  incompetence *ability*
inaccessible unreachable, out-of-the-way,
  unapproachable, out of reach *accessible*
inaccurate incorrect, inexact *accurate*
inactive idle, sluggish, motionless, still, calm
  active
inadequate deficient, lacking, wanting, short
  of, insufficient, unsatisfactory *enough,
  adequate*
inappropriate unfitting, unsuitable,
  improper *appropriate*
inattentive unmindful, heedless, unobserving,
  distracted, negligent, wandering *attentive*
inaugurate begin, install, introduce, launch,
  admit, initiate, instate
inborn natural, innate, hereditary, instinctive
incapable unable, incompetent, unqualified,
  unfit *capable*

incense　1 provoke, anger, annoy, irritate, vex, exasperate, ruffle, pique;　2 fragrance, perfume, aroma, scent

incentive　motive, stimulus, encouragement, inducement

incessant　continual, uninterrupted, unbroken, constant, ceaseless, endless, nonstop, infinite, perpetual, steady　*interrupted*

incident　happening, event, occurrence, experience, adventure

incipient　beginning, initial, introductory　*final*

incite　stir, urge, rouse, agitate, excite, inflame, provoke, instigate

incline　1 tend, be willing, be game;　2 influence, affect, sway, move, induce, persuade;　3 lean, bend, bow, tilt, tip;　4 slope, hill, grade

include　contain, comprise, cover, enclose　*exclude*

income　receipts, returns, profits, earnings, proceeds, wages　*payment*

incomparable　matchless, unequalled　*comparable*

incompetent　unable, incapable, unqualified, unfit　*competent, able*

incomplete　unfinished, deficient, wanting, lacking, imperfect, partial　*complete*

incomprehensible　unintelligible, hard to understand, difficult, vague, obscure　*understandable*

inconceivable　unbelievable, unthinkable, unconvincing, incredible　*believable*

inconsiderate　thoughtless, unmindful　*considerate*

inconsistent　disagreeing, illogical, unreasonable, senseless, invalid　*consistent*

inconspicuous　unseen, unnoticed, unapparent　*conspicuous*

inconvenient untimely, inappropriate, unfavourable, troublesome, awkward *convenient, timely*

incorporate join, unite, combine, unify, merge

incorrect wrong, faulty, inaccurate, improper *correct, right*

increase enlarge, extend, add to, expand, advance, raise *decrease*

incredible unbelievable, doubtful, questionable, unconvincing, staggering, preposterous, absurd, ridiculous *believable*

indebted owing, obliged, involved

indeed in fact, in truth, really, absolutely, positively, perfectly, certainly, definitely, surely, of course

indefinite unclear, vague, indistinct, obscure, confused, hazy, general, broad *definite*

indelible permanent, indestructible, unforgettable, fixed

independent acting alone, unconnected, unassociated, self-reliant *dependent*

indescribable unexplainable, extraordinary, exceptional, remarkable *ordinary*

index list, chart, file, table, sign, symbol, guide

indicate show, point out, exhibit, demonstrate, display, present, express, suggest, hint, imply, signify

indifferent unbiased, impartial, detached, disinterested, cool, neutral, impersonal, unconcerned *concerned*

indigenous native, original, natural to *foreign*

indignant angry, irate

indignity insult, affront, offense, injury *respect*

indirect devious, roundabout, out-of-the-way *direct*

indiscreet unwise, imprudent, unsound, unreasonable, ill-advised *careful*

indispensable essential, necessary, needed, required, vital *unnecessary*

indisposed 1 ill, sick, ailing *well*; 2 unwilling, forced *willing*

indistinct unclear, confused, dim, obscure, vague, cloudy, hazy, blurred *clear, distinct*

individual 1 single, separate, one, personal, special; 2 human, man, being

indolent lazy, shiftless, do-nothing, unenterprising, slothful *ambitious*

indomitable unconquerable, unyielding, invincible, unbeatable, uncontrollable, unruly, unmanageable *yielding, controllable*

induce influence, persuade, lead on, cause, elicit, evoke, prompt, move, sway

induct introduce, bring in, install, place, inaugurate, enlist, enroll, draft

indulge humour, favour, oblige, please, gratify, satisfy, cater to, pamper, coddle, spoil

industrious hard-working, diligent, energetic, tireless *lazy*

industry trade, business, manufacture, labour, work, concern, dealings

inedible uneatable *edible*

ineffectual useless, ineffective, powerless, unsuccessful *effective*

inefficient unable, incapable, incompetent, unfit, inept, unskilful *efficient*

inequality unevenness, irregularity, imbalance *equality*

inert lifeless, slow, sluggish, motionless, inactive, stagnant, listless *active*

inevitable destined, fated, doomed, unavoidable, sure, certain, inescapable

inexcusable unpardonable, unforgivable, unjustifiable *excusable*

inexpensive cheap, low-priced, reasonable *expensive*

inexperienced unpractised, untried, green, unfamiliar, ignorant, immature, undeveloped *experienced*
inexplicable unexplainable, mysterious *understandable*
infallible reliable, sure, unerring, right *unreliable*
infamous wicked, bad, disgraceful, evil, base, low, shameful, notorious, terrible, scandalous, outrageous *virtuous, good, moral*
infancy beginning, babyhood *maturity*
infantry army, foot soldiers
infect 1 disease, contaminate, communicate, pollute, corrupt, poison; 2 influence
infer 1 conclude, reason, deduce, gather, derive, assume, presume, suppose, expect, reckon, calculate, imagine; 2 indicate, imply, suggest, hint
inferior lower, worse, subordinate, secondary, lesser *superior*
infest overrun, crawl with, plague, beset
infinite limitless, boundless, endless, immeasurable, perpetual, everlasting, eternal, ceaseless *limited*
infirm weak, feeble, unstable, sickly, unsound, frail *strong, healthy*
inflame 1 excite, stir, move, affect, provoke, arouse, incite, anger *soothe, calm*; 2 redden, swell, irritate
inflate swell, puff out, expand, broaden, enlarge, stretch, increase, blow up *deflate*
inflexible stiff, rigid, firm, unbending, unyielding, stubborn, inelastic *flexible*
inflict give, cause, impose, effect, produce, bring about, wreak
influence sway, affect, move, induce, persuade, prejudice

inform 1 tell, communicate, advise, enlighten, instruct, notify, report

infrequent rare, scarce, sparse, scattered, occasional, uncommon, irregular *frequent*

infringe violate, break, trespass, overstep

infuriate enrage, anger, madden, antagonize, provoke, irritate, incite, agitate *soothe, calm*

infuse 1 put in, instil; 2 inspire, lift, infect, animate; 3 drench, saturate, bathe

ingenious clever, skilful, proficient, masterful, inventive, original, creative, imaginative, productive, inspired *unoriginal, dull*

ingenuous 1 frank, open, sincere, candid, straightforward *secretive*; 2 simple, natural, innocent, plain, unsophisticated *sophisticated*

inhabit live, dwell, occupy, reside, lodge, stay, room

inhale breathe in, gasp, sniff, smell *exhale*

inherent internal, natural, implanted, existing, belonging, instinctive

inherit receive, come into

inhospitable uncordial, unfriendly, unreceptive, ungracious, unneighbourly *friendly, hospitable*

inhuman unfeeling, cruel, brutal, ruthless, uncivilized *kind*

iniquity injustice, evil, sin, wrong, crime, outrage *justice*

initial 1 first, earliest, beginning, primary, introductory *final*; 2 first letter

initiate 1 start, begin, originate, pioneer, lead, head, institute, introduce, launch, break the ice; 2 admit, receive, take in, install, let in *expel*; 3 instruct, introduce, educate

inject force into, fill, insert *extract*

injure damage, harm, hurt, wound, wrong, impair *heal*

injustice inequity, unfairness, unjustness
  justice
inmate occupant, resident, tenant, inhabitant
inmost 1 deepest, farthest in; 2 private, secret
innocent 1 guiltless, faultless, blameless,
  sinless *guilty*; 2 harmless *harmful*
innovate introduce, change, modernize
innumerable countless, many, infinite,
  unlimited *few*
inoculate immunize, vaccinate
inoffensive harmless, unobjectionable
  offensive
inquire ask, question
inquisitive curious, prying, snooping,
  meddlesome
insane crazy, foolish, mad, unbalanced,
  deranged *sane*
insatiable greedy, unquenchable, covetous
inscribe write, engrave, mark, imprint,
  impress, stamp
insensible unfeeling, unaware, unconscious,
  numb, unknowing *sensitive, aware*
insert put in, enter, introduce, inject, set in
  extract
inside 1 in, into, within; 2 interior, innermost
insight wisdom, perception, intuition
insignia emblems, badges, symbols
insignificant unimportant, meaningless,
  negligible, small, little, slight *significant,*
  meaningful
insincere dishonest, false, superficial,
  artificial *sincere*
insinuate hint, suggest, imply, intimate,
  indicate
insist urge, press, maintain, stress, demand
insolent rude, insulting, impudent, arrogant,
  haughty, defiant, bold *polite*
insoluble unexplainable, unsolvable *soluble*

inspect   examine, observe, study, contemplate

inspire   influence, cause, prompt, encourage
discourage

install   1 admit, establish, let in, inaugurate,
instate, receive;   2 place, put in, fix, plant,
set

instance   example, case, occasion,
circumstance

instant   1 immediate, pressing, urgent, prompt,
quick;   2 moment, second

instead   in place of, rather than, in lieu of

instinct   natural feeling, natural tendency

institute   1 establish, begin, set up, create,
organize, form, launch;   2 society,
organization, school, establishment,
foundation

instruct   1 teach, educate, show, guide;
2 inform, direct, tell, command, order, dictate,
advise

instrument   tool, device, means, implement,
utensil, apparatus, gadget, appliance,
contraption

insufficient   inadequate, not enough,
unsatisfactory, deficient   *enough*

insulate   isolate, separate

insult   offend, affront, humiliate

insure   1 protect, safeguard, defend, shelter,
cover;   2 guarantee, warrant, assure,
endorse, certify, sponsor, back

insurgent   rebel, rioter, revolter, agitator,
ringleader, troublemaker, instigator, rabble-
rouser

insurrection   revolt, rebellion, mutiny, riot,
uprising   *obedience, compliance*

intact   untouched, whole, uninjured,
undamaged, unchanged, complete

intake   1 input, entry;   2 income, earnings,
revenue, receipts, proceeds, profits

intangible untouchable, insubstantial
tangible

integrate 1 equalize, balance, coordinate,
proportion; 2 amass, form a whole
segregate

integrity 1 honesty, sincerity, uprightness,
honour, respectability *dishonesty*;
2 wholeness, completeness, totality
incompleteness

intelligent sensible, bright, knowing,
understanding, rational, aware, perceptive
ignorant

intend mean, plan, propose, aim, have in mind,
contemplate

intense 1 great, considerable, extreme,
drastic; 2 forceful, strong, dynamic, fierce,
severe, rigorous *moderate*

intercede go between, interfere, intervene,
mediate, negotiate, arbitrate, umpire, referee

intercept interrupt, check, stop, arrest, hold
up

interchange exchange, change, switch, trade,
substitute

intercourse 1 communication, dealings;
2 sexual relations, copulation

interest 1 concern, curiosity, intrigue
unconcern, apathy; 2 share, portion, part,
percentage; 3 premium, rate, profit;
4 business, affair, matters

interesting arousing, provocative, inviting,
entertaining, thought-provoking, fascinating,
absorbing, gripping, engrossing, enthralling,
spellbinding, captivating, intriguing,
attractive, appealing *uninteresting, dull*

interfere 1 intervene, intercede, mediate,
arbitrate, umpire, referee; 2 meddle, intrude,
encroach, interrupt

interior inside, inner, middle, heart, core,
nucleus *exterior, outside*

interlude   intermission, interval, interim, respite, break, pause, recess, interruption

intermediate   in between, intervening, middle

interminable   endless, long, lengthy, infinite, perpetual

intermingle   mix, blend, merge, combine, mingle   *separate*

intermission   pause, interruption, interlude, interval, interim, respite, break, recess

intermittent   periodic, recurrent, sporadic, irregular, broken, unsteady   *regular, continual*

internal   inner, inside, interior, innermost   *external, outer*

interpret   explain, clarify, translate, analyze

interrogate   question, examine, quiz, test, inquire of, grill, cross-examine

interrupt   break in, hinder, stop, intrude, interfere

interval   interruption, intermission, interlude, interim, respite, break, pause, recess

intervention   interference, intrusion, infringement, meddling

interview   question, interrogate, quiz, test, examine

1. intimate   1 close, familiar;   2 innermost, private, secret

2. intimate   hint, suggest, imply, indicate, insinuate

intimidate   frighten, threaten, menace, cow, browbeat, bully, harass, terrorize

intolerable   unbearable, insufferable   *tolerable, bearable*

intolerant   impatient, unsympathetic, bigoted, prejudiced   *tolerant, understanding*

intoxicated   1 drunk, inebriated   *sober*;   2 excited, impassioned, moved, touched, impressed, affected   *unmoved*

intrepid fearless, dauntless, brave, courageous, bold, valiant, heroic *timid, afraid*

intricate complicated, perplexing, entangled, complex, confused, involved *simple*

intrigue 1 plot, scheme, conspiracy; 2 love affair, romance, amour

intriguing fascinating, alluring, captivating, charming, enchanting, enthralling, attractive, interesting, appealing, enticing, inviting, tantalizing, thrilling, tempting, provocative *unappealing, dull*

introduce 1 bring in, inaugurate, institute, launch, innovate; 2 present, acquaint with

intrude interfere, infringe, encroach, trespass, meddle, overstep

inundate flood, overflow, run over, cascade, deluge, drench

invade intrude, overrun, encroach, trespass, advance upon, infringe, raid, attack

invalid 1 sickly, weak, unhealthy, infirm, frail, debilitated; 2 void, without value, ineffective *valid*

invaluable priceless, precious, dear, worthwhile *worthless*

invariable unchanging, constant, permanent, unalterable, uniform, steady, consistent *changing*

invent originate, make up, devise, develop, contrive, concoct

inventory stock, collection, list

invert turn around, reverse

invest 1 venture, stake; 2 empower, place, provide, endow

investigate search, explore, examine, inspect, study, scrutinize, review, probe

invigorating stimulating, exhilarating, energizing, refreshing, bracing *debilitating, weakening*

invincible unbeatable, unconquerable,
  invulnerable, impregnable *vulnerable*
invite 1 ask, request, call, summon; 2 attract,
  tempt, interest, appeal
invoke pray, beseech, entreat, beg, implore,
  appeal, plead
involuntary 1 unwilling, forced;
  2 instinctive, automatic, mechanical,
  spontaneous, reflex, unconscious, compulsive,
  unthinking, unintentional *voluntary*
involve 1 include, concern, affect, entail,
  implicate, encompass, envelop;
  2 complicate, tangle, confuse, confound;
  3 occupy, absorb, engross
irate angry, mad, indignant, infuriated
irksome tiresome, tedious, wearisome,
  troublesome, bothersome, trying, annoying,
  irritating
irregular 1 unnatural, abnormal; 2 unenven,
  erratic, distorted, rough *regular*
irrelevant unfitting, inappropriate, unrelated,
  far-fetched *relevant*
irresistible compelling, moving
irresolute hesitating, uncertain, unsure,
  indecisive, fickle *resolute, definite*
irreverent disrespectful, discourteous,
  insolent, impudent, impious *respectful*
irritable impatient, cross, cranky, irascible,
  testy *pleasant, agreeable*
irritate 1 annoy, vex, incite, agitate, stir up,
  provoke, instigate, foment, infuriate, madden,
  anger; 2 make sore, pain, hurt, wound,
  chafe, rub, grate *soothe*
isolate separate, segregate, set apart,
  quarantine, seclude
issue 1 cause, principle, campaign, problem,
  topic, subject, theme, text, question, point;
  2 publication, edition, copy

item 1 part, segment, portion, subdivision, component, piece, article; 2 notation, entry

itemize list, sum up, total, summarize

J

jagged pointy, ragged, notched, serrated *smooth*

jail imprison, lock up, hold captive, incarcerate

jam 1 crowd, stuff, load, cram, press, squeeze, push, crush, heap; 2 jelly, marmalade, preserve

jealous envious, desirous of, covetous

jeer make fun of, taunt, scoff, mock

jeopardize risk, endanger, imperil, hazard, expose

jetty breakwater, pier, buttress, bulwark

job work, business, employment, task, assignment, duty, position

jog run, trot, gait, sprint, lope

join connect, fasten, clasp, unite, combine, couple, link, put together, attach, annex *separate, part, detach, disconnect, disjoin*

joke jest, quip, banter, tease

jolly merry, cheerful, pleasant, joyful, jovial, gleeful *sad, solemn, grim, serious, glum*

jostle push, shove, thrust, bump

journal 1 daily record, account, log, diary, chronicle; 2 newspaper, magazine

journey trip, voyage, tour, expedition, excursion, jaunt, outing

jovial kindly, good-natured, merry, good-hearted, good-humoured, joyful, gleeful, jolly *sad, solemn, grim, serious, glum*

jubilant rejoicing, exulting, triumphant, overjoyed, gay, delighted, elated *dejected*

judge 1 decide, consider, form an opinion; 2 mediate, referee, umpire

judicious wise, sensible, thoughtful, well-advised *ignorant*

jumble mix, confuse, scramble, muddle *compose, arrange, organize*

jump spring, leap, bound, vault, hurdle, hop

junction joining, connection, union, linking, coupling, meeting, hookup, tie-up *separation*

junior 1 younger; 2 lower, lesser, secondary, subordinate, minor *senior*

junk 1 rubbish, trash, scrap, litter, debris; 2 Chinese sailing ship

just 1 exact, precise; 2 only, merely; 3 righteous, fair, proper, good, moral, virtuous *corrupt, unjust*

jut stick out, project, stand out, protrude *recess, indent*

juvenile young, youthful *old, mature, aged*

K

keen 1 sharp, cutting, fine, acute; 2 quick, exact, smart, bright, clever, sharp-witted *dull*

keep have, hold, maintain, preserve, conserve, save, tend, protect, guard *discard, lose*

key 1 opener; 2 clue, answer, explanation, lead; 3 tone, pitch, note

kid 1 tease, joke, fool, jest; 2 child, tot; 3 young goat

kidnap snatch, carry off, abduct, shanghai

kill slay, slaughter, murder, destroy, end, finish, annihilate, execute

kind 1 friendly, gentle, decent, generous, considerate, warm-hearted, tender, sympathetic, thoughtful *mean, cruel, unkind*; 2 sort, type, variety, species, nature, make

kindle 1 set afire, light, ignite *extinguish*;
2 arouse, stir up, start, trigger, move,
provoke *calm, pacify*

king ruler, sovereign, monarch, chief,
potentate

kit equipment, set, outfit, furnishings, gear, rig

knack skill, talent, art, know-how

knave rascal, tricky man, rogue, scoundrel,
villain

knead mix, blend, combine, massage

knock hit, strike, punch, job, pound, beat,
hammer, rap, bang

know understand, comprehend, perceive,
recognize, identify, be sure of, be aware

L

label name, title, tag

labour work, toil, employment, industry

labyrinth maze, complex, tangle

lack want, need, require, fall short

lacquer varnish, polish, gild

laden loaded, burdened, weighted

lament mourn, sorrow, grieve, bewail,
bemoan *rejoice, celebrate*

lance pierce, cut, puncture, stab, perforate,
knife, impale

land 1 ground, soil, sod, shore, surface, earth;
2 descend, arrive, touch down, alight

landmark point, milestone

lane path, road, narrow way, pass, aisle, alley,
avenue, channel, artery

language speech, words, tongue, talk

languid weak, drooping, feeble, debilitated,
listless, lethargic, dull, sluggish *energetic,
vigorous*

lapse sink, decline, slump, go down

larceny theft, stealing, robbery

large big, sizable, great, grand, huge, vast, immense, enormous, colossal, giant, gigantic, mammoth, massive *small, little*

lark fun, fling, joke, spree, celebration, revel

lash strike, blow, beat, hit, whip, flog

last latest, end, final, conclusive, ultimate *first, beginning*

latch hook, clasp, lock, fastener, catch, closing, seal

late behind, slow, tardy

latent hidden, concealed, covered, obscured, underlying

latter later, more recent *former*

laud praise, commend, glorify, compliment, extol *belittle, criticize*

laugh giggle, chuckle, smile, grin, titter, guffaw, howl, roar

launch start, set afloat, introduce, fire, set going, spring

lavatory bathroom, loo, toilet, latrine, washroom

lavish free abundant, liberal, plentiful, ample, extravagant, generous, prodigal *stingy, sparing, skimpy*

law rule, principle, standard, formula, ordinance, regulation, act, decree, proclamation, edict

lax loose, slack, careless, lenient, vague, lazy *rigid, firm*

lay put, place, set, rest, deposit, arrange

lazy lax, inactive, indolent *active, ambitious*

lead come first, head, escort, guide, conduct, direct, run

league union, alliance, association, society, federation, group, band

leak drip, dribble, run out

lean 1 thin, scant, spare, lanky, meagre, slight, slim, slender, narrow, skinny, scrawny *bulky, fat*; 2 bend, rest, slope, slant, incline, tip

leap jump, spring, vault, hop, bound, hurdle, dive, plunge, pounce

learn memorize, gain knowledge, discover, find out

lease rent, hire, let, charter

least fewest, smallest, minimum *most, maximum*

leave go, depart, quit, abandon, withdraw, vacate, exit *arrive, stay*

lecture speech, talk, sermon, address, recitation, discourse, oration

ledge shelf, ridge, edge, rim

legal lawful, legitimate, authorized, permitted, allowed, admissible, valid, sound, just *illegal*

legend story, fiction, fairy tale, myth, fable, folklore

legible readable, plain, clear *illegible*

legion unit, outfit, regiment, troop, battalion, company, squad, team, division, army, force

legislation lawmaking, resolution, regulation, ruling, enactment, decree, ordinance, statute

legitimate lawful, rightful, allowed, legal, authorized, permitted, admissible, valid, sound, just *illegitimate*

leisure freedom, spare time

lend give, loan, advance

length extent, measure, span, reach, stretch, distance

lenient mild, gentle, merciful, lax, loose, relaxed, unrestrained, soft, easy *harsh, strict*

less smaller, fewer, reduced *more*

lesson teaching, instruction, assignment, exercise, course, study

let 1 allow, permit, leave, consent, grant, admit *deny*; 2 rent, lease, hire out, charter, contract

letter 1 alphabet sign, character, symbol; 2 message, note, communication, dispatch

level flat, even, equal, uniform, constant, steady, smooth *uneven*

liable 1 likely, probable, apt; 2 responsible, accountable, answerable

liar fibber, falsifier, fabricator, perjurer, storyteller

liberal 1 generous, plentiful, abundant, ample, extravagent, lavish, extensive, unselfish *stingy*; 2 tolerant, broadminded, freethinking, progressive *conservative*

liberty freedom, independence, autonomy, emancipation

license permit, warrant, consent, authorization, sanction, approval

lie 1 fib, falsify, fabricate, exaggerate; 2 recline, repose

life existence, being

lift raise, pick up, elevate, hoist

light 1 bright, clear, open, lucid *dark*; 2 weightless, airy, delicate *heavy*

like prefer, care for, be fond of, fancy, enjoy, appreciate *dislike*

likeness similarity, resemblance *difference*

likewise similarly, also, moreover, too, as well

limit end, boundary, restriction, extreme, tip, confine

limp weak, drooping, sagging, flimsy, loose, soft, floppy *stiff*

line 1 rope, cord, wire, string; 2 mark, stroke, stripe, streak, dash; 3 edge, boundary, limit, confine; 4 row, arrangement, series, sequence; 5 type, kind, brand, sort, make

linger stay, wait, delay, remain, tarry, loiter, dawdle, dillydally, lag

link unite, connect, join, combine, couple, put together, bridge *separate*

liquid fluid *solid*

liquor whisky, drink, alcohol, spirits

list 1 enumeration, schedule, record, register, inventory, line-up; 2 tilt, tip, slant, slope, lean

listen hear, eavesdrop

literally exactly, actually, really, word-for-word

literate learned, scholarly, cultured, educated *illiterate*

literature writings, books, publications

litter clutter, rubbish, trash, scrap, rubble, debris, junk

little small, short, tiny, bit, minimum, slight, miniature, mini, puny, teeny, wee *big*

live 1 be alive, exist *die*; 2 reside, occupy, dwell, stay, house, room, inhabit

livelihood support, keep, maintenance, sustenance, subsistence

lively exciting, bright, cheerful, vivid, vigorous, gay, active, energetic, interesting, spirited, animated, vivacious, spry *dull*

livestock cattle, animals

livid 1 pale, greyish; 2 very angry, furious, enraged

load 1 burden, pack, cargo, freight; 2 fill, stuff *unload, empty*

loan lend, advance, give

loathe hate, dislike, abhor, detest, abominate, despise *love*

local regional, limited, particular, restricted

location position, place, region, area, zone, territory, district, section, neighbourhood, spot, site, situation

lock fasten, close, hook, clasp, latch, shut, seal *unlock, open*

locomotion travel, movement, motion, transit

lofty high, grand, dignified, proud, haughty,
eminent, prominent, elevated, soaring,
towering

logical reasonable, sensible, sound, sane,
rational *illogical, unreasonable*

loiter linger, idle, stop, dillydally, wait, delay,
stay, tarry, dawdle

lonely alone, solitary, isolated,
unaccompanied, friendless, desolate

long lengthy, extensive, far-reaching *short*

look 1 see, search, hunt, explore, stare, glance,
peek, peer, gaze, gape, gawp; 2 seem, appear

loose 1 limp, drooping, slack, unfastened,
untied *tight*; 2 vague, free, unclear,
confused, hazy, inexact *definite*

lose 1 fail, flop, be unsuccessful, forfeit,
sacrifice *win, succeed*; 2 misplace, mislay
find

lot 1 many, bunch, group, cluster, clump
few; 2 quantity, amount, sum, number,
portion; 3 fate, fortune, chance, luck,
destiny, end; 4 field, plot, tract

lottery raffle, draw

loud noisy, thunderous, roaring, resounding
soft, low

love adore, like, care for, be fond of, fancy,
idolize, cherish *hate*

lovely delightful, exquisite, charming,
appealing, enchanting, beautiful, pretty,
attractive, fetching

low 1 inferior, lesser, short *high*; 2 mean,
coarse, vulgar, base, wicked, evil, bad, sinful,
vile

loyal true, faithful, obedient, dutiful, devoted,
trustworthy *disloyal*

luck chance, fortune, fate, lot, fortuity

ludicrous ridiculous, absurd

lull   quiet, calm, hush, silence, stillness, pause, rest, break, recess, intermission, respite, lapse, letup

luminous   light, shining, radiant, beaming, gleaming, glowing, bright, clear

lump   swelling, bump, mass, hunk, chunk

lure   pull, attract, draw on, entice, seduce

lurid   terrible, sensational, startling, melodramatic

lurk   hide, sneak, slink, prowl, creep

luscious   delicious, savoury, pleasing, tasty

luxury   extravagance, frills, prosperity, elegance, comfort, well-being, magnificence, grandeur, splendour, swankiness   *poverty*

M

mad   1 crazy, insane, wild, foolish, lunatic, daft, demented, deranged, unbalanced, touched   *sane*;   2 angry, annoyed, irritated, exasperated, disgruntled, enraged, furious, cross, irritable, raging, disagreeable *peaceful*

magazine   journal, periodical, publication

magic   witchcraft, wizardry, sorcery, voodoo

magnetic   attractive, pulling, drawing, alluring

magnificent   splendid, grand, stately, majestic, superb, exquisite, marvellous, wonderful, grandiose, glorious, imposing, elaborate, impressive

magnify   exaggerate, increase, intensify, expand, enhance, enlarge, extend, broaden, stretch, inflate   *minimize*

maim   cripple, disable, injure, hurt, wound

main   chief, most important, principal, foremost, leading, dominant, primary, first *secondary*

maintain   keep, uphold, possess, support, bear, sustain, preserve, save, guard, protect, retain

majestic grand, stately, noble, great, kingly, dignified, high, prominent, eminent, regal, royal, imperial, sovereign, grandiose, magnificent, impressive, elegant, imposing, proud

major larger, greater, superior, higher, senior *minor*

make 1 build, form, shape, compose, create, assemble, manufacture, fashion, fabricate, construct, produce, do, execute *destroy*; 2 cause, force, compel; 3 kind, brand, type, line, sort

manage control, conduct, handle, direct, operate, work, regulate, govern, lead, supervise, administer, run

mandate command, order, dictate, injunction, referendum

manoeuvre operate, work, run, conduct, handle, drive, manipulate, engineer, plot, scheme, intrigue, conspire, plan

mania craze, insanity, madness, infatuation, enthusiasm, desire

manipulate handle, manage, touch, feel, operate, work, conduct, manoeuvre

man-made artificial, not natural *natural*

manner way, kind, mode, style, fashion, form, nature, character, means, method

manslaughter killing, homicide, murder, assassination, elimination

manual 1 guidebook, directory, handbook; 2 by hand

manufacture make, invent, create, fashion, construct, build, erect, compose, prepare, devise, fabricate

many numerous, various, multitudinous, myriad, several, considerable *few*

map chart

marathon race, relay, contest

margin border, edge, rim, leeway, room
mark 1 line, sign, evidence, indication, manifestation; 2 grade, rating
marked noticeable, plain, evident, noted, apparent, decided
martial militant, warlike, military, combative, belligerent, aggressive, hostile *peaceful*
martyr sufferer, victim, tortured
marvellous wonderful, extraordinary, miraculous, astounding, superb, magnificent, glorious, divine, exceptional, remarkable
mask disguise, cover, camouflage
mass bulk, lump, quantity, load, amount, measure, volume, accumulation, hunk, chunk, lots, pile, stack, heap
massacre slaughter, killing, butchery, carnage, pogrom
massage rub, knead, stroke
massive big, large, heavy, solid, sturdy, strong, clumsy, ponderous, thick, coarse *little, small*
masterly expert, skilful, proficient, adept, handy, clever
match 1 lighter; 2 contest, battle, engagement, encounter, game, sport, play; 3 duplicate, twin, double, companion, mate, fellow, counterpart, complement, equivalent, equal
material substance, fabric, stuff, matter, composition, goods
maternal motherly *paternal, fatherly*
mathematics numbers, measurements, figures, calculation, computations
matrimony marriage, wedding, nuptials
matter 1 material, substance, composition, content; 2 affair, business, concern, transaction, activity
mature ripe, full-grown, developed, mellow, adult, ready *immature*

maxim proverb, rule, law, code, regulation, principle, adage, saying

maximum largest, highest, greatest, uppermost, head, chief *minimum*

may be able, can, be allowed

maybe possibly, perhaps, conceivably, perchance

meal repast, spread

mean 1 signify, intend, denote, imply, indicate, suggest, connote; 2 petty, unkind, malicious, ill-humoured, cross, irritable, testy *pleasant*; 3 average, medium, normal, middle

measure size, grade, rank, compare, assess, appraise, estimate, rate

medal award, honour, reward, medallion, prize

meddle interfere, busybody, intrude, interrupt, intervene, trespass

mediate make peace, settle, negotiate, intercede, intervene, referee, umpire, arbitrate

medicinal healing, helping, relieving, remedial, corrective, therapeutic

mediocre average, ordinary, fair, moderate, adequate, satisfactory, acceptable, passable, so-so

meditate think, reflect, consider, contemplate, study, ponder, weigh, brood, deliberate

medium 1 middle, average, mean, halfway, mediocre, fair; 2 instrument, tool, agent, implement

meet join, unite, connect, come together, assemble, gather, encounter, converge *separate*

melancholy sad, gloomy, blue, pensive, wistful, depressing, dismal *cheerful*

member part, offshoot, branch, organ

memorable notable, rememberable

memorandum   note, letter, report, reminder, memo

memorize   learn by heart, remember

menace   threat

mend   repair, improve, fix, service, patch up, heal   *break, impair*

mention   remark, comment, observe, say, note, state, name, specify, stipulate, designate

merchandise   goods, wares, commodities, products

mercy   kindness, compassion, pity, sympathy, charity

merge   absorb, swallow, combine, unite, mix, blend, fuse, join, mingle, scramble   *separate*

merit   quality, value, worth, goodness, excellence, fineness

merry   gay, joyful, jolly, jovial, gleeful, mirthful, festive   *sad, downcast*

message   word, communication, dispatch, letter, epistle, note

meteoric   swift, flashing, brief, blazing

method   system, way, manner, means, mode, fashion, style, procedure, process, form, course, plan, scheme, design, arrangement

metropolitan   city, civic, urban, municipal

microscopic   infinitesimal, tiny, minute   *huge*

middle   centre, heart, core, nucleus, hub

mighty   strong, powerful, great, grand, potent, majestic, forceful, vigorous, stout, sturdy, rugged, robust, hearty   *weak*

migrant   roving, travelling, wandering, roaming, rambling, meandering, drifting, straying, transient   *stationary*

mild   gentle, kind, calm, warm, temperate, moderate, lenient, good-natured, good-humoured   *harsh, violent*

militant   fighting, warlike, combative, belligerent, aggressive, hostile, antagonistic, contentious, pugnacious, bellicose   *peaceful*

military army, troops, soldiers, armed forces, service

mimic imitate, copy, ape, mock, mime, parrot, copycat

mind 1 brain, intelligence, mental ability, intellect; 2 obey, heed, regard, comply, listen to *ignore*; 3 attend, watch, observe, notice, look after

minimum least, lowest, smallest *maximum*

minister clergyman, spiritual guide, pastor, chaplain

minor 1 smaller, lesser, inferior, secondary, lower *major*; 2 underage, immature

minus less, lacking, without, excepting, missing, absent

1. minute instant, moment, twinkling

2. minute small, tiny, miniature, slight, negligible, insignificant *large, significant*

miraculous wonderful, marvellous, remarkable, extraordinary, phenomenal, incredible, awesome

mirror reflect, echo, copy, imitate

miscellaneous mixed, combined, blended, conglomerate, scrambled, jumbled

miserable poor, mean, wretched, unhappy, pitiful, shabby, woeful, sorry *happy*

misfortune difficulty, trouble, distress, hardship, ruin, mishap, disaster, catastrophe, calamity, tragedy, accident *good fortune, good luck*

misgiving doubt, suspicion, anxiety, question, scepticism, qualm, concern, uneasiness

misjudge mistake, err, slip up, miscalculate

mislead deceive, misdirect, misinform

miss fail, lose, forfeit, sacrifice *get, succeed*

missile rocket, projectile

missing lacking, wanting, lost, absent, nonexistent, vanished, gone

mission   errand, business, purpose, task, work, stint, job, assignment, chore, charge, duty

mistake   error, blunder, fault, slip, oversight, faux pas

mistrust   doubt, be sceptical, suspect, distrust, question, challenge, dispute   *trust*

misunderstanding   disagreement, difficulty, difference, misinterpretation, mistake, error   *understanding*

mix   stir, join, blend, combine, fuse, mingle, merge   *separate*

moan   wail, groan, howl, cry, bawl, suffer, agonize, complain

mob   crowd, mass, throng, multitude, horde, pack, bunch

mobile   movable, changeable, fluid   *immobile*

mock   mimic, imitate, ape, ridicule, scoff, jeer, taunt, deride, laugh at

model   copy, shape, design, reproduction, duplicate, replica, standard, prototype, image, likeness

moderate   calm, fair, medium, mild, conservative, temperate, gentle, restrained, lenient   *extreme, harsh*

modern   contemporary, up-to-date, progessive, forward-looking   *archaic*

modest   humble, bashful, shy, quiet, unpretentious, plain, simple   *showy*

modify   change, alter, vary, diversify, qualify, adjust, fix

moment   instant, minute, twinkling

momentum   force, impetus, thrust, push

money   currency, legal tender, cash

monopoly   control, corner, possession

monotonous   boring, humdrum, repetitious, tedious, dreary, dull   *interesting*

monstrous   horrible, dreadful, shocking, grotesque, deformed, disfigured

monument   tower, memorial, shrine, pillar

mood   feeling, temperament, humour, disposition, nature, frame of mind, phase

moody   gloomy, sullen, glum, mopish, morose, sulky *cheerful*

moral   right, just, ethical, honourable, reputable, respectable, law-abiding, virtuous, good, righteous *immoral*

morale   spirit, enthusiasm

morbid   1 unhealthy, sickly, diseased, unwholesome *healthy*; 2 ghastly, horrible, dreadful, awful, shocking, appalling *pleasant*

more   greater, further, farther, in addition, extra, another *less*

moreover   besides, also, furthermore, as well, too

mortal   1 human being, person, soul, individual, body; 2 deadly, fatal, lethal, killing, destructive, malignant

most   greatest, extreme, maximum, supreme, highest, majority *least*

mother   1 originate, produce, cause, bring about, breed; 2 female parent, mummy, mama, mum *father*; 3 care for, attend to, look after, watch, mind, foster, nurse, nurture

motion   1 movement, stir, activity, proceedings, doings; 2 suggestion, proposal, legislation, resolution, proposition

motive   reason, cause, ground, basis, motivation, prompting

motto   saying, maxim, proverb, adage

mould   1 shape, form, sculpture, carve, model; 2 decay, rot, spoil, deteriorate, disintegrate, crumble, go bad

mount   1 rise, get on, ascend, go up, climb, board *descend*; 2 increase, gain, grow, advance *decrease*; 3 position, place, fix, set *remove*

mourn grieve, sorrow, lament, bewail, bemoan *rejoice*

move 1 change, budge, stir, stimulate, impel, motivate, animate; 2 influence, sway, affect, persuade, induce, arouse, prompt, convince

much quantity, abundance, volume, mass

mud mire, muck, slush, slime, dirt

muddle mess, disorder, confusion, chaos

muffle silence, mute, dull, soften, deaden, cushion, smother, stifle, suppress

muggy warm, damp, close, stuffy, humid, dank, sticky

multiply increase, advance, gain, grow, rise, procreate

mumble mutter, speak indistinctly *shout*

municipal civic, urban, metropolitan

murder 1 kill, assassinate, eliminate, purge, liquidate, slaughter, massacre; 2 spoil, ruin, botch, muff, mar, butcher, make a mess

muscle strength, brawn

musical melodious, tuneful, lyrical, dulcet, harmonious

must should, ought to, be obliged to, have to, need to, be forced to

muster assemble, gather, collect, summon, cluster, accumulate, amass, group, compile, recruit *scatter, disperse*

mutilate cut, tear, break off, amputate, clip, lacerate

mutiny rebellion, revolt, riot, insurrection, uprising, insurgence

mutual reciprocal, joint, common

mysterious secret, hidden, profound, mystical, recondite, occult

mystify bewilder, puzzle, perplex, baffle, confound

myth legend, story, fiction, fantasy, fable, fairy tale, falsehood, fabrication *truth*

N

nag 1 pester, annoy, bother, pick on; 2 horse, pony

naked uncovered, exposed, nude, bare, undressed *covered*

name title, label, tag, appellation

narrow slender, close, tight, restricted, cramped, confined, meagre, limited *wide*

nasty unpleasant, revolting, disgusting, repulsive, offensive, foul, vile, sickening, nauseating, filthy, odious, obnoxious, dirty

nation country, land, society, community

native natural, original, indigenous *foreign*

natural genuine, typical, real, authentic, legitimate, honest, pure, original, true, characteristic, normal *unnatural, false*

naturally of course, plainly, certainly, surely, indeed

naughty bad, disobedient, misbehaving, disorderly, evil, wrong

near close, imminent, at hand *far*

nearly almost, close to, just about, approximately

neat 1 clean, orderly, trim, tidy, shipshape, well-kept *disorderly, sloppy*; 2 skilful, clever, apt, adept, proficient, handy, expert, materful, well-done

necessary required, compulsory, urgent, important, imperative, obligatory, compelling, needed, essential, exigent *unnecessary*

need want, lack, require

neglect overlook, disregard, ignore, pass over, slight, be inattentive, be careless, be thoughtless, be inconsiderate *care*

negotiate arrange, talk over, settle, mediate, intervene, umpire, arbitrate, referee

neighbouring   near, bordering, next to, adjoining, adjacent, surrounding

nervous   excited, upset, restless, disturbed, ruffled, shaken, flustered, agitated, perturbed, high-strung, tense, strained, edgy, jittery *calm, composed*

net   1 trap, snare;   2 lacelike cloth, mesh, web;   3 gain, earn, acquire, get, obtain, secure

neutral   impartial, detached, unprejudiced, cool, independent, indifferent   *involved*

nevertheless   however, notwithstanding, although, but, regardless, anyway

new   fresh, modern, recent, original, young, unused, firsthand   *old*

news   tidings, information, word, story

next   following, nearest, closest, succeeding, successive, subsequent

nice   pleasing, agreeable, satisfactory, enjoyable, desirable, gratifying, good, fine

nimble   light, quick, active, fast, swift, speedy, agile   *slow*

noble   great, grand, majestic, distinguished, lofty, eminent, prominent, important, grandiose, magnificent, stately, dignified, aristocratic   *common*

noise   sounds, racket, clamour, din, clatter, uproar, tumult, bedlam, hubbub, commotion, ballyhoo, rumpus   *quiet*

nomad   wanderer, traveller, rover, roamer, vagrant, migrant

nomination   naming, appointment, selection, choice, designation

nonsense   foolishness, ridiculousness, folly, absurdity, stupidity, rubbish, poppycock

normal   usual, regular, average, standard, ordinary, typical, characteristic, true to form   *abnormal, unusual*

notable striking, important, remarkable, noteworthy, memorable, special, extraordinary, exceptional, rare, famous, distinguished, renowned, celebrated, well-known, prominent, popular, notorious

note 1 write, record, inscribe, list, mark down, jot down, indicate, mark, comment; 2 observe, heed, regard, notice

notice note, observe, heed, regard, see

notify announce to, inform, advise, report, tell, instruct, remind, warn

notorious famous, renowned, celebrated, popular, well-known, infamous

nourish feed, nurture, nurse, strengthen, sustain, maintain

novel new, original, fresh, unique, firsthand, different, unusual

now 1 at once, immediately, right away *later*; 2 presently, today, at this time

nucleus middle, core, heart, kernel, hub, focus

nuisance annoyance, pest, bother, trouble, irritation

numb dull, unfeeling, deadened, insensitive

number 1 quantity, sum, count, collection, amount, measure, bulk, portion, multitude; 2 numeral, figure, digit, symbol

numerous many, multitudinous, several, abundant, various, myriad, considerable *few*

nurse nurture, nourish, foster, feed, sustain, care for, tend to, mind

nurture rear, bring up, foster, train, care for, raise, feed, tend, mind, nurse, nourish

nutrition food, nourishment

O

oath promise, pledge, vow, agreement, commitment, bond

obey yield, submit, comply, mind, heed, listen to *disobey, resist*

object 1 thing, article; 2 purpose, end, goal, target, intent, aim

objection protest, challenge, dissent, disapproval, complaint, criticism *approval*

obliging helpful, considerate, thoughtful, accommodating, well-meaning *discourteous*

obscene dirty, smutty, filthy, lewd, bawdy, pornographic, unclean, indecent *decent, clean*

obscure indistinct, unclear, indefinite, faint, dim, vague, dark, shadowy, blurred, fuzzy, hazy *clear*

observe 1 see, note, examine, study, perceive, behold, inspect, scrutinize, contemplate, review; 2 celebrate, commemorate; 3 keep, practise, obey, comply with, heed, follow *neglect, ignore*

obsolete extinct, passé, old-fashioned, dated, outmoded, discontinued, antiquated *recent, stylish*

obstacle barrier, obstruction, block, stoppage, hindrance, deterrent, impediment, hitch, snag, catch

obstinate stubborn, wilful, headstrong, bullheaded, pig-headed, unyielding, unbending, inflexible, adamant, firm, stiff, rigid *flexible*

obstruct block, hinder, clog, bar, impede, delay *aid, help*

obtain get, acquire, gain, secure, procure, earn, receive *lose*

obvious plain, understandable, apparent, clear, evident, manifest, explicit, distinct *hidden*

occasionally sometimes, now and then, once in a while, from time to time

occupant tenant, resident, lodger, inhabitant, dweller, boarder

occupation 1 business, employment, trade, work, activity, affair, matter, concern, interest, capacity, role, function, duty, task, stint, job; 2 possession, holding, ownership

occur happen, take place, transpire, come about

odd 1 strange, peculiar, queer, unusual, curious, unique, eccentric, weird, bizarre *usual, ordinary*; 2 extra, left over, remaining, spare

offend displease, hurt, pain, grieve, wound, disgust, sicken, horrify, affront, insult *please*

offer present, propose, suggest, submit, try, attempt

office 1 position, duty, task, job, work, function, capacity, role, post; 2 room, workplace, headquarters, studio, department

often repeatedly, many times, frequently *seldom*

old 1 aged, ancient, antique, elderly, mature *young, new*; 2 former, obsolete, abandoned, discontinued, stale, outworn, discarded *recent*

old-fashioned outdated, outmoded, unfashionable *stylish*

omen sign, indication, warning, portent

ominous threatening, unfavourable, sinister, menacing

omit neglect, exclude, leave out, bar, miss, skip *include*

one-sided partial, unfair, prejudiced, biased *neutral, impartial*

only just, merely, simply

onset 1 beginning, commencement, start, opening *end*; 2 attack, assault, offense, charge, drive, onslaught

onward further, forward, ahead *backward*

open 1 begin, start, launch, initiate, unfold, establish, originate *close*; 2 expose, uncover, disclose, reveal, show, bare *cover*

openly frankly, sincerely, freely *secretly*

operate work, run, manage, conduct, carry on, handle, function, perform, act

opinion belief, judgment, estimate, impression, feeling, sentiment, attitude, view, theory, conception, thought, idea, outlook, conviction

opponent enemy, foe, adversary, competitor, rival, combatant, contender *ally, friend*

opportunity chance, occasion, time, opening, turn, spell

oppose fight, struggle, resist, hinder, contradict, conflict with, counteract, refute, dispute, cross *agree*

oppressive harsh, severe, unjust, burdensome, overbearing, domineering, dictatorial, tyrannical

optimistic cheerful, happy, bright, pleasant, radiant, glad, lighthearted, jaunty, carefree *pessimistic*

optional voluntary, elective *required*

oral spoken, voiced, vocalized, sounded, articulated, verbal, uttered, said

orbit path, circuit, circle, revolution, route

ordeal experience, test, trial, tribulation

order 1 arrangement, condition, state, manner, mode, way, disposition, formation, system; 2 command, bid, direction, instruction

ordinary 1 usual, common, normal, average, regular, everyday, standard *unusual, special*; 2 mediocre, inferior, poor, so-so *outstanding, exceptional*

organize arrange, classify, systematize, categorize, sort, group, set up, establish, orient

origin 1 beginning, start, infancy, birth, inception; 2 source, parentage, derivation, root

orthodox usual, customary, conventional, traditional, accepted, proper, correct *unorthodox, different*

other different, distinct, additional, extra, supplementary, further, fresh, new

ought should, be obliged, must, need to, have to

outbreak revolt, riot, disturbance, uprising, rebellion, eruption, outburst, torrent

outburst eruption, outbreak, torrent, discharge, ejection

outcast homeless, friendless, abandoned, deserted, forlorn, forsaken, derelict, rejected, disowned

outcome result, consequence, effect, upshot, fruit, conclusion

outcry noise, clamour, uproar

outdo surpass, excel, outshine, defeat, beat

outfit equip, furnish, prepare, rig, fit

outing trip, journey, jaunt, excursion

outlaw outcast, exile, criminal, convict

outlay spending, expense, costs

outline 1 plan, sketch, diagram, chart, draft, pattern, drawing; 2 profile, contour, skeleton

outlook view, attitude, position

outlying remote, external, outer

outnumber exceed

output yield, production, proceeds, crop, harvest

outrageous shocking, insulting, absurd, nonsensical, ridiculous, foolish, crazy, preposterous, bizarre, excessive, extreme, exorbitant, disgraceful, shameful, scandalous, unwarranted

outright altogether, entirely, completely, thoroughly, wholly, fully, totally, quite, freely, openly, downright

outset start, beginning, commencement, opening

outspoken frank, unreserved, unrestrained, open, vocal, candid, straightforward, direct, forthright *shy, reserved*

outwit outmanoeuvre, outdo, outsmart

overcast cloudy, dark, gloomy, dismal, sombre, bleak, hazy, misty *clear, bright*

overcome conquer, defeat, upset, overpower, surmount

overflow flood, run over, cascade, spill, inundate

overhaul repair, service, mend, fix, condition

overhead 1 above, high, aloft; 2 cost, expense

overjoyed delighted, enchanted, ecstatic, elated, enraptured, jubilant *depressed*

overlook 1 neglect, ignore, disregard, pass over, skip, let slip, miss *note, notice*; 2 face, view, watch

overpower master, overwhelm, surmount, defeat, conquer, crush, vanquish

overrun exceed, spread, infest, beset, abound, flood

oversee supervise, manage, direct, superintend, administer, preside, boss

oversight error, slip, negligence, omission

overthrow defeat, destroy, overcome, overpower, overturn, upset, unseat, dethrone

overwhelm 1 crush, overcome, defeat, surmount, conquer, vanquish; 2 astonish, surprise, amaze, astound, bewilder, startle, dumbfound, flabbergast

owe be indebted, be obliged, be liable

own have, possess, hold, maintain, monopolize

P

pace 1 rate, speed; 2 stride, gait, step, walk, tread

pacify quiet, calm, tranquilize, soothe, appease, placate, mollify *anger, provoke*

pack fill, load, stuff, cram, stow, box *unpack, empty*

pact agreement, contract, understanding, bargain, treaty, alliance

page 1 paper, sheet, leaf; 2 attendant, usher, errand boy, servant

pain suffering, hurt, discomfort, distress, ache, pang, soreness, irritation

paint 1 coat, colour, cover, decorate, trim, garnish; 2 draw, sketch, picture, depict, draft, portray, represent

pair set, two, couple, both, twins, mates, team, duo

palace castle, mansion, villa, chateau

pale dim, colourless, faint, weak, vague, indistinct, lifeless pallid, wan, sallow, whitish *bright, vivid*

pamphlet booklet, brochure, leaflet, folder

panel 1 group, forum, board; 2 partition, wall, division, separation, barrier

panic fear, fright, scare, alarm, dread, awe, terror, phobia

panorama scene, vista, lookout, sight

par average, normal

parade procession, show, display, review, promenade, march, exhibition, pageant

paradise heaven, bliss, glory, ecstasy, elation, enchantment

paralyse deaden, numb, desensitise, disable, cripple

parcel package, bundle, pack, lot

pardon forgive, excuse, absolve, exonerate, exculpate, acquit, vindicate

park 1 land, reservation, sanctuary; 2 settle, place, put, set, station

part 1 portion, segment, fraction, share, division, section, component, cut; 2 role

participate partake, contribute, take part in, have a hand in, enter into, join in

particular 1 special, unusual, different *ordinary*; 2 meticulous, critical, discriminating, fastidious, finicky, exacting, fussy

parting departure, going away, leaving, exit, withdrawal *arriving*

partition separation, division, wall

partner companion, mate, collaborator, assistant, participant, comrade, colleague

party 1 group, company, gang, crew, body, band, faction; 2 person, individual, fellow; 3 festival, fete, affair, ball, celebration

pass 1 succeed, do well *fail*; 2 spend, use, employ; 3 deliver, hand over, transfer; 4 go, travel, move, progress

passage 1 corridor, hallway, arcade, entranceway, opening, lane, channel, artery, passageway; 2 section, paragraph, chapter, excerpt, selection, extract; 3 voyage, cruise, crossing, trip, trek

passion 1 emotion, strong feeling, fervour, craze, enthusiasm; 2 rage, anger, fury, violence; 3 love, affection, fondness, ardour, lust, desire

passive inactive, dormant, submissive, unresisting, compliant, yielding, docile, mild, gentle *forceful*

past ended, gone by, former, over, previous, preceding *future*

pastime recreation, amusement, enjoyment, diversion, relaxation

patch mend, repair, fix, service

paternal fatherly *maternal, motherly*

path　route, track, way, trail, road, line

pathetic　pitiful, touching, moving, sad, distressing

patience　tolerance, endurance, indulgence, perseverance, persistence　*impatience*

patriotic　loyal, nationalistic, chauvinistic

patrol　watch, guard, protect, keep vigil, police

patronize　1 deal with, trade with;　2 back, sponsor, finance, promote, support

pattern　1 arrangement, design, illustration, picture, print;　2 model, example, standard, prototype, paragon

pause　wait, stop, rest, recess, cease

pay　give, remunerate, compensate

peaceful　quiet, calm, still, tranquil, placid, untroubled, pacific, serene, cool　*troubled*

peak　top, crest, hilltop, summit, pinnacle, crown, tip, apex, acme, zenith

peculiar　1 strange, odd, unusual, queer, curious　*ordinary*;　2 special, distinctive, characteristic, typical, representative

pedestrian　walker, hiker

peel　strip, pare, skin

peer　1 equal, match, equivalent, like;　2 look, peek, peep

pen　1 write, inscribe, record;　2 enclose, confine, shut in, surround, coop up

penalize　punish, chastise, discipline, castigate

pending　waiting, until, during

penetrate　1 pierce, enter, puncture, bore, perforate;　2 understand, perceive, see through

penniless　poor, destitute, down-and-out, bankrupt

pension　allowance, aid, assistance, help, subsidy, grant, stipend

people　persons, folks, community, society, public, human beings

perceive   sense, observe, feel, experience, detect, recognize, distinguish, make out

percentage   proportion, part, ratio, rate, quota

perennial   continuous, constant, perpetual, steady, regular

perfect   faultless, flawless, ideal, correct, accurate, right   *imperfect, faulty*

perforate   pierce, penetrate, puncture, enter, bore

perform   do, act, execute, transact, carry out, accomplish, achieve

perhaps   possibly, maybe, conceivably

peril   danger, harm, jeopardy, hazard, risk, endangerment

period   interval, span, time

perish   die, decrease, succumb, disappear, vanish, decay

permanent   lasting, durable, enduring, long-lasting, unchanging, constant, stable, steady   *temporary*

permit   allow, consent, let, grant, admit

perpendicular   upright, vertical

perpetual   eternal, lasting, continuous, unceasing, permanent, infinite, endless, incessant, constant   *short-lived, brief*

perplex   puzzle, bewilder, baffle, confound, mystify

persecute   harm, oppress, torment, harass, molest, torture, antagonize, badger

persevere   persist, endure, continue, carry on, keep on

persist   last, stay, continue, endure, prevail, go on, persevere

person   individual, soul, somebody, someone

personal   private, special, individual, specific, particular   *impersonal*

personality   identity, individuality

perspire   sweat

persuade convince, convict, convert, win over, induce *dissuade*

perverse 1 stubborn, contrary, wilful, difficult, obstinate; 2 wrong, incorrect, untrue, false, erroneous; 3 wicked, corrupt

perverted distorted, twisted, warped, contorted *normal*

pessimistic unhappy, cheerless, joyless, gloomy, cynical *optimistic, cheerful*

petition request, demand, requisition, appeal, plea

petty 1 unimportant, small, trivial, puny, minor, inferior *important*; 2 mean, base, low, wretched, miserable, despicable, contemptible

phase stage, state, aspect

philanthropic charitable, kindly, benevolent, bighearted, generous, giving, humanitarian *selfish, stingy*

photograph snap, film, take a picture

phrase clause, part, section, passage

pick choose, select, harvest, gather, cull

picket 1 strike, boycott, revolt; 2 bar, fence, wall, enclose

picnic feast, outing, festivity

picture represent, illustrate, portray, depict, describe, characterize

piece part, bit, portion, division, segment, section, share

pier dock, wharf, breakwater

pierce penetrate, puncture, perforate, stab, bore

pile heap, stack, mound, collection

pilgrimage journey, trip, trek, expedition, crusade

pillar column, support, shaft, monument, post

pin clasp, fasten, hook, clip

pioneer settler, leader, colonist, forerunner

pious religious, devout, reverent, faithful, believing *atheistic*

pit hole, cavity, crater, hollow

pitch 1 throw, fling, hurl, toss, sling, cast, heave; 2 sway, fall, topple, flounder, stagger, rock, roll, reel, lurch; 3 tar

pitfall trap, snare

pity sympathy, sorrow, compassion, mercy

place arrange, fix, compose, put, locate, situate, set, station

placid calm, peaceful, quiet, still, tranquil, smooth, pacific, untroubled

plague 1 disease, epidemic, pestilence; 2 annoy, vex, bother, torment, molest, trouble, harass, badger, worry, pester, haunt *soothe, comfort*

plain 1 clear, understandable, simple, distinct, obvious, evident *complex, involved*; 2 homely, ordinary, unattractive *pretty*

plan propose, intend, design, mean, aim, think, devise, arrange, plot, scheme, manoeuvre, project

plane 1 flat, level, horizontal, even, smooth *uneven*; 2 aeroplane, aircraft

plant establish, fix, root, settle, sow

plastic changeable, variable, mobile, fluid, flexible, pliant, supple *rigid, fixed*

platform 1 stage, rostrum, balcony; 2 policy, programme, plan, course

playful frisky, sportive, gay, spirited, lively, animated, vivacious, frolicsome, impish, mischievous *serious, solemn*

plea 1 request, appeal, petition, asking; 2 excuse, defence

pleasant pleasing, enjoyable, likeable, desirable, agreeable, gratifying, delightful, charming, appealing, enchanting, cheerful, genial, happy, satisfying *unpleasant, displeasing*

pledge   promise, vow, oath, assurance, guarantee, word

plentiful   ample, enough, abundant, generous, sufficient, lavish   *scarce, insufficient*

plot   1 plan, scheme, intrigue, conspire, contrive, manoeuvre, concoct;   2 outline, sketch, graph, map, chart, blueprint, diagram

plug   block, clog, stop, obstruct, stuff, jam, congest

plump   fat, round, stuffed, stout, obese, fleshy, corpulent, pudgy, chubby, stocky, chunky, tubby   *thin*

plunder   rob, steal, loot, pillage, fleece

plunge   dive, plummet, drop, fall, swoop down

plush   luxurious, sumptuous, elegant, elaborate, grand, magnificent, glorious, impressive, majestic

pocket   load, pack, stow, take in, accept, receive, take, get, acquire

poetry   verse, rhyme, lyric, ode

point   direct, aim, show, indicate

poised   composed, collected, balanced, confident, assured   *upset*

poisonous   toxic, deadly, destructive, noxious, harmful, malignant, venomous

police   guard, watch, patrol, shield

policy   plan, programme, procedure, course, principles, line, platform

polish   shine, burnish, gloss, rub, buff, glaze, wax

polite   refined, courteous, civil, gracious, respectful, well-mannered, tactful   *rude*

poll   canvass, survey, vote, questionnaire

pollute   contaminate, infect, taint, tarnish, defile, foul, poison

pomp   spectacle, display, sight, exhibition, show, pageant, ostentation, magnificence   *modesty*

pool 1 lake, pond, puddle, reservoir;
2 contribute, combine

poor 1 needy, penniless, impoverished,
destitute *rich*; 2 pitiful, unfortunate,
wretched, miserable *fortunate*

popular 1 common, usual, regular, customary,
ordinary, everyday, prevalent, conventional,
traditional *unusual*; 2 well-liked, dear,
beloved, adored, admired, cherished,
favourite, pet *unpopular, disliked*

population inhabitants, people

port harbour, dock, wharf, pier

portion part, share, division, segment, section,
fraction, fragment, piece *whole*

portray represent, picture, depict, illustrate,
characterize, impersonate, describe

pose 1 posture, position, bearing, carriage;
2 pretence

position 1 place, location, situation, spot;
2 job, duty, function, role, office, capacity,
situation, post

positive sure, definite, certain, absolute,
convinced, assured

possess own, have, hold, control, maintain,
occupy

possible likely, conceivable, imaginable,
feasible, probable, credible, achievable,
attainable, plausible *impossible*

post 1 list, schedule, notify, inform;
2 position, situation, office, duty, job

postpone delay, put off, defer, suspend, hold
over, table, shelve, stall, procrastinate

potent powerful, strong, forceful, mighty
weak, puny

potential possible, promising, hidden, likely,
conceivable

pounce jump, swoop, leap, spring, hop, bound,
hurdle, vault, plunge, dive

power strength, might, force, vigour, energy, potency, authority, control, influence, command, mastery, dominion

practically 1 usefully, profitably, advantageously; 2 almost, nearly, really, essentially, fundamentally, basically, about

practise train, drill, exercise, prepare, condition, rehearse, repeat

praise compliment, commend, laud, approve of, extol, glorify, flatter

pray appeal, plead, petition, beg, entreat, implore, beseech

precaution forewarning, notification

precede lead, head, come first, forerun *follow, succeed*

precinct district, boundary, limit, community, vicinity, neighbourhood

precious valuable, expensive, costly, dear, loved, priceless, adored, cherished, admired, prized, special *cheap*

precipice bluff, cliff, slope

precise exact, accurate, definite, careful, strict, positive, absolute, meticulous, detailed, explicit, clear-cut

precocious advanced, forward, premature

predecessor leader, forerunner

predicament mess, complication, plight, embarrassment, pinch, dilemma

predict foresee, foretell, prophesy, divine, forecast, portend

predominant chief, superior, main, principal, leading, foremost

prefer choose, favour, rather, desire, fancy, pick, select

pregnant productive, fertile, full

prejudiced biased, opinionated, partial, influenced *impartial*

preliminary prior, preceding

premature   early, advanced, forward, too soon, hasty   *late, delayed*

premeditated   planned, forethought, intended, plotted, calculated, meant, deliberate   *spontaneous, accidental*

prepare   ready, fix, arrange, provide, concoct, compose, equip, rig, plan

prescribe   order, direct, assign, advise, recommend, suggest, advocate

presence   attendance, being, existence, occurrence, appearance

present   give, offer, tender, submit, extend, donate, bestow, award, grant, deliver, hand over

preserve   protect, keep, maintain, guard, defend, save, shelter, shield, screen, harbour, uphold, support, reserve, conserve, sustain, retain   *destroy, neglect*

press   1 push, force, squeeze, clasp, tighten; 2 urge, insist, coax, goad, prod, stress; 3 iron, smooth

pressing   urgent, compelling, crucial, necessary, driving

prestige   importance, greatness, distinction, prominence, significance, superiority, mastery, power, influence, authority

presume   suppose, assume, surmise, guess, think, imagine, fancy, imply, infer

presumptuous   daring, bold, arrogant, insolent, brazen   *modest, humble*

pretend   make-believe, act, feign, bluff, sham, fake

pretentious   showy, ostentatious, flashy, fancy, affected   *modest*

pretty   attractive, lovely, beautiful, handsome, good-looking   *ugly*

prevent   prohibit, forbid, deter, keep from, preclude, stop, block, thwart, inhibit, hinder   *allow, permit*

previous prior, earlier, former, one-time, preceding *following, succeeding*

price cost, value, amount, rate, charge, worth, expense

priceless valuable, invaluable, precious, dear, expensive, costly

pride self-respect, self-esteem, dignity, vanity, egotism

primary first, important, chief, main, principal, leading, dominant, essential, basic, fundamental, foremost, paramount *secondary*

primitive 1 ancient, original, prehistoric, uncivilized, barbarous, native *modern*; 2 simple, basic, fundamental, elementary, beginning *advanced, sophisticated*

principal chief, main, important, leading, dominant, foremost, primary, head, prominent, essential *secondary*

principle rule, law, standard, belief, dogma, doctrine, truth, proposition, precept

prior earlier, before, previous, former *after, later*

prison jail, penal institution, penitentiary, reformatory

privacy secrecy, seclusion, intimacy, retreat, hideaway, sanctum, cloister, withdrawal, isolation, solitude

privilege advantage, license, favour, liberty, freedom, grant

prize 1 reward, award, treasure; 2 value, appreciate, hold dear, cherish, adore, idolize, worship, respect, revere

probable likely, liable, apt, presumable, promising, hopeful *improbable*

probation test, trial, try, check

problem issue, question, mystery, enigma, puzzle, perplexity, conundrum

procedure process, course, measure, custom, practice, rule, policy, plan, method, way, manner, means

proceed progress, advance, go forward, go ahead

proceeds receipts, income, profits, earnings, returns

process operation, procedure, course, step, act, way, manner, means, mode

productive fruitful, fertile, yielding, prolific, creative, inventive, gainful, profitable *sterile*

professional occupational, vocational

proficient skilled, expert, adept, apt, clever, masterful, ingenious, deft, effective, competent, crack *inefficient, clumsy*

profit gain, benefit, advantage, earnings, returns, receipts, proceeds *loss*

programme schedule, plan, list, prospectus, calendar, agenda, roster, register, line-up, bill

progress advance, proceed, go ahead, move

prohibit forbid, bar, ban, disallow, veto, deny, prevent, deter, thwart, restrict, foil *allow*

1. project plan, scheme, proposal, plot, design, intention, undertaking, enterprise, venture

2. project 1 protrude, stick out, bulge *recede*; 2 show, screen

prolific productive, rich, plentiful, fruitful, creative *sterile*

prolong extend, stretch, lengthen, elongate, drag out *shorten*

prominent well-known, important, outstanding, distinguished, great, eminent, famous, popular, celebrated *unknown*

promising hopeful, encouraging, favourable, probably *hopeless*

promotion advancement, forwarding, improvement, lift, rise, betterment, progress

prompt 1 punctual, quick, instant, immediate, ready *slow, late*; 2 remind, hint, suggest, coach

prone 1 inclined, liable, willing, ready *unwilling*; 2 flat, level, horizontal, prostrate, reclining, reposing *vertical, standing*

pronounced distinct, marked, decided, plain, clear, obvious, evident, definite, clear-cut, visible, downright, absolute, conspicuous, noticeable, prominent, bold, striking, outstanding, flagrant, glaring *unnoticeable, vague*

prop support, bolster, hold up, brace

propel drive, push, shove, move, impel, motivate, stimulate

proper correct, right, fitting, decent, respectful, accurate, perfect, faultless, tasteful *improper, unsuitable*

property possession, holdings, belongings

prophesy predict, foretell, forecast, divine, foresee, soothsay

proportion ratio, measure, amount, balance, portion, share, interest, part, percentage

proposal plan, scheme, suggestion, offer, intent, project, design, motion

prosecute 1 complete, carry out, fulfil, discharge, execute, transact, practise, exercise, pursue, follow; 2 bring suit, take action against

prospective expected, anticipated, awaited, coming, promised, due, future, eventual

prosperous successful, thriving, fortunate, triumphant, comfortable, flourishing, well-off, wealthy, rich, opulent, affluent *unsuccessful, poor*

protect defend, guard, shield, safeguard, shelter, screen, cover, ensure, harbour

protest object, squawk, dispute, challenge, dissent *agree*

proud 1 boastful, dignified, elated, pleased, satisfied, gratified, delighted; 2 arrogant, haughty, vain, lofty, conceited, bragging *humble, modest*

prove show, verify, check, confirm, justify, certify, establish, substantiate, demonstrate, document

provide supply, give, furnish

province 1 division, department, part, field, sphere, domain; 2 region, area, zone, territory, district, quarter, place, neighbourhood, kingdom, empire, principality

provoke anger, vex, excite, stir, irritate, annoy, incense, exasperate, pique, ruffle, enrage, infuriate, antagonize, irk, nettle, disturb, arouse, taunt, aggravate, peeve, rile *pacify, soothe*

prowl sneak, slink, lurk, steal, creep, rove

prudent careful, sensible, discreet, cautious, guarded, judicious *careless*

pry 1 meddle, mix, busybody, peek, peep, search, grope, snoop; 2 loosen, jimmy, wrench

public people, populace, society, persons, population, inhabitants

puffy swollen, inflated, bloated, distended, dilated *deflated*

pull 1 tug, draw, heave, haul, tow, drag, yank, jerk, strain, stretch *push*; 2 attract, lure, influence

punch pummel, beat, thrash, flog, strike, pound, hammer, rap, bang, batter, wallop

punctual prompt, quick, immediate, speedy, exact, precise *late*

punish discipline, chastise, correct, castigate, penalize

pupil student, scholar, schoolchild

purchase buy, shop
purify cleanse, clarify, clean, clear, refine, filter *soil, pollute*
purpose plan, aim, intention, design, object, goal, target, resolution, determination, will
pursue chase, follow, seek, go after, shadow, trail, heel, hunt, quest
push 1 press, thrust, shove, force, drive, propel, nudge *pull*; 2 urge, encourage, prod, coax, spur, goad *discourage*
put place, lay, set, arrange, deposit *remove*
puzzle perplexity, quandary, dilemma, confusion, bewilderment, mystery, enigma, problem, conundrum

Q

quake shake, tremble, vibrate, quiver, shiver, shudder
qualified competent, fit, capable, efficient, able, suited, eligible *unfit, unsuitable*
quality nature, kind, characteristic, constitution, trait, feature, mark, type, property
quantity amount, number, sum, measure, portion, volume, mass, multitude
quarantine separate, segregate, isolate, confine, seclude
quarrelsome argumentative, cranky, cross, irritable, peevish, belligerent, grouchy *peaceful*
queer 1 odd, strange, peculiar, curious, eccentric, weird *normal*; 2 homosexual, deviant
query question, ask, inquire, demand, interrogate, quiz *answer*
quest search, hunt, pursue, seek, explore

question inquire, ask, query, demand, interrogate, quiz *answer*

questionable doubtful, uncertain, dubious, improbable, unlikely, implausible *certain, sure*

quick 1 fast, swift, hasty, brisk, lively, speedy, rapid, fleet, expeditious; 2 alert, attentive, smart, bright, keen, sharp *slow*

quiet still, silent, hushed, peaceful, serene, tranquil, calm *noisy*

quit stop, leave, cease, discontinue, end, halt, desist, refrain, depart, withdraw, retreat, abandon, resign, vacate *continue, remain*

quite completely, absolutely, entirely, really, truly, rather, very, exceedingly

quiz test, examine, interrogate, question, query

quota ratio, share, proportion, percentage, allotment

quote cite, illustrate, refer to, repeat, echo

R

race 1 run, speed, rush, tear, dash, dart, hurry, hasten, scoot, scamper, scurry, sprint, bound, bolt, quicken, accelerate, chase; 2 people, folk, clan, tribe, nation, breed, culture, lineage

radical extreme, greatest, utmost, fundamental

radio broadcast, transmit

rage 1 anger, passion, violence, storm, frenzy, furore, fit, delirium, mania, craze, excitement *calm, serenity*; 2 fad, fashion, style

ragged torn, worn, shabby, shoddy, tattered, frayed, frazzled, seedy *neat*

raid attack, invade, assult, plunder, pillage, loot, seize

raise 1 lift, increase, elevate, hoist, boost *lower*; 2 produce, rear, build, create, construct *destroy*

rally 1 assemble, meet, gather, congregate, collect, throng, crowd, cluster, convene *disperse*; 2 improve, recover, recuperate, mend, revive

rampage racket, commotion, hubbub, tumult, uproar, disturbance, fracas, ado, fuss, rumpus, stir, row *peace, quiet*

random haphazard, aimless, irregular, unorganized *planned*

range limit, extent, distance, reach, length, scope

rank 1 grade, class, position, rate, value, evaluate, gauge, appraise, classify, arrange, group, categorize; 2 offensive, repulsive, disgusting, revolting, foul, vile, odious, repugnant, obnoxious, sickening, nasty, putrid, rotten *fresh, wholesome*

ransack search, rummage, forage, pillage, plunder, loot, raid, rifle

ransom redeem, reclaim, recover, retrieve, regain

rapid quick, swift, fast, speedy, fleet, hasty, expeditious *slow*

rare scarce, sparse, uncommon, infrequent, peculiar, unusual *common, ordinary*

rash 1 hasty, careless, reckless, impetuous, impulsive, sudden, imprudent, brash *careful, cautious*; 2 inflammation, breaking-out

rate grade, classify, position, rank, value, evaluate, appraise, group, categorize, estimate, measure

ratio proportion, comparison, percentage

ration allowance, portion, share, quota, allotment, budget, measure, supply, amount

rational sensible, reasonable, thinking, logical, sound, level-headed *irrational, foolish*

rattle 1 clatter, patter; 2 confuse, disturb, upset, fluster, ruffle, unsettle *calm*

ravishing enchanting, delightful, lovely, appealing, charming, beautiful, stunning, dazzling, gorgeous, alluring, enticing, fascinating *unattractive, plain*

raw 1 immature, inexperienced, green, undeveloped, callow, crude *developed, experienced*; 2 cold, wind-swept, nippy, wintry, freezing, piercing, bitter *warm, mild*; 3 uncooked *cooked*

raze destroy, tear down, level, flatten, demolish *build, construct*

reach 1 arrive at, come to, approach, land; 2 extend, stretch

react respond, answer

ready prepared, set, fit *unprepared*

real actual, true, genuine, authentic, substantial, certain, legitimate, bona fide, sincere, honest, pure *untrue, fake*

realize understand, grasp, conceive, comprehend, follow, appreciate

rear 1 back, hind, posterior *front*; 2 raise, produce, create, nurse, foster, train

reason cause, motive, explanation, logic, sense, ground, justification, basis

reasonable sensible, fair, logical, just, sound, sane, rational, practical, realistic, justifiable *unreasonable*

rebel revolt, rise up, defy, riot, mutiny, disobey, disregard *obey*

recall 1 remember, recollect, review, reminisce *forget*; 2 summon, call back

receive take in, get, gain, admit, accept, obtain, secure *give*

recent new, late, modern, up-to-date

reception party, entertainment, social, festivity

recipe   formula, instructions, directions, prescription

reckless   rash, careless, heedless, thoughtless, inconsiderate, hasty, unmindful, impetuous *cautious, careful*

reckon   1 think, consider, judge, suppose, hold, regard, deem, imagine, fancy, believe; 2 count, calculate, compute, estimate, figure, evaluate, appraise

recognize   1 acknowledge, see, behold, know; 2 realize, appreciate, understand, admit, allow, accept

recollect   remember, recall, reminisce, review, reflect

recommend   advise, suggest, advocate, instruct, guide, direct, urge

recompense   pay, reward, compensate

reconcile   settle, harmonize, bring together, mend, fix up

record   write, inscribe, register, enrol, list, mark down, note, post, enter, log, tabulate, chronicle

recover   1 regain, retrieve, get back, reclaim, rescue *lose*; 2 recuperate, get better, rally, revive, heal, improve, come around, make a comeback, get back in shape

recreation   play, amusement, entertainment, pleasure, enjoyment, diversion, relaxation, pastime, fun, sport *work, toil*

recruit   enlist, draft, sign up, enrol, muster

rectify   adjust, remedy, fix, regulate, set right, amend, correct

recur   repeat, return, come again

reduce   lessen, lower, decrease, diminish, cut, moderate *increase*

refer   direct, point, recommend, send, allude

referee   judge, moderator, umpire, arbitrator, mediator

reflect 1 mirror, send back; 2 think, ponder, study, deliberate, consider, contemplate, meditate, muse, mull over

reform change, improve, convert, revise

refrain avoid, abstain, forego, shun *indulge*

refuge shelter, protection, asylum, retreat, haven, port, harbour, sanctuary

refund repay, reimburse, pay back

1. refuse decline, reject, say no, rebuff *accept, allow*

2. refuse waste, garbage, rubbish, rubble, trash, litter, junk

regal 1 royal, majestic, sovereign, imperial; 2 dignified, stately, splendid, magnificent, imposing

regardless notwithstanding, despite

region place, space, area, location, district, zone, territory, section, vicinity

register record, inscribe, write, enrol, list, post, enter, log, indicate

regret bemoan, bewail, be sorry for, rue

regular 1 usual, customary, steady, habitual, everyday, common, typical, normal, routine; 2 uniform, even, orderly, balanced, symmetrical *irregular*

regulate 1 manage, govern, handle, direct, rule, control, organize, run, command; 2 adjust, remedy, rectify, correct

rehearse practise, repeat, train, drill, exercise, prepare

reinforce strengthen, fortify, brace, intensify *weaken*

reject exclude, bar, eliminate, expel, discard, throw away, dispose of, cast off, refuse, decline *accept*

relapse return, revert, regress, reverse, slip back *advance*

related associated, connected, affiliated, allied, akin

relax   rest, east up, loosen

relay   carry, deliver, pass, transfer, hand on, impart

release   free, let go, relieve, dismiss, discharge, expel, fire, sack, retire, relinquish, liberate *hold*

relent   yield, bend, give, relax, submit, give in

relentless   harsh, without pity, merciless, unsympathetic, ruthless, heartless, cruel, strict, firm, rigid, inflexible, unyielding, uncompromising, persevering, persistent, steadfast, hard *lenient, sympathetic*

relevant   pertinent, applicable, apropos, suitable, connected, fitting *unconnected, irrelevant*

reliable   trustworthy, dependable, faithful, steadfast, loyal, true, devoted, safe, sure, stable *undependable, unreliable*

relief   1 freedom, ease, alleviation, release, help, assistance, aid; 2 change, substitution, replacement, alternate, proxy

religious   pious, devout, reverent, faithful

reluctant   unwilling, grudging, disinclined, loath *willing*

rely   depend on, trust, confide, count on

remain   continue, endure, persist, stay, last, keep on *leave, depart*

remark   comment, speak, state, say, observe, note, mention

remarkable   unusual, noteworthy, extraordinary, exceptional, wonderful, marvellous, great, striking, notable, special, rare *ordinary*

remedy   cure, correct, fix, rectify, heal, treat, doctor

remember   remind, recall, recollect, recognize *forget*

remind   prompt, suggest to

remote far, distant, removed, secluded, isolated, hidden *near, close*

remove take away, withdraw, extract, eject, expel, oust, deduct, subtract, eliminate, dispose of, doff, discard *keep*

rendezvous meeting, appointment, session, get-together

renounce give up, relinquish, surrender, yield, waive, abandon, release, reject, deny, disclaim, discard, spurn, scorn *keep*

renowned famous, celebrated, popular, distinguished, notable, notorious, well-known *obscure, unknown*

rent hire, lease, charter, let

repair mend, fix, service, overhaul, patch up, restore *break, destroy*

repeat say again, recite, reiterate, duplicate, echo

repel 1 drive back, rebuff, hold off; 2 repulse, offend, revolt, disgust, nauseate, sicken *attract*

replica copy, reproduction, duplicate, double

reply answer, respond, retort, acknowledge, react

report describe, tell, repeat, relate, narrate

represent 1 portray, depict, illustrate, stand for, symbolize, characterize, express, describe; 2 exhibit, show, demonstrate, display, manifest, present, reveal, disclose

repress keep down, restrain, suppress, quell, crush, squash, smother, stifle, hush up, censor, muffle

reprove scold, blame, lecture, reprimand, chide, rebuke

reputable honourable, respectable, well-thought of, upstanding, upright, principled, moral, honest *dishonest*

request ask, requisition, apply for

require　1 need, necessitate, lack, want;
　　2 demand, order, command, oblige

rescue　save, free, recover, redeem, salvage,
　retrieve, release, liberate, extricate

research　investigate, inquire, hunt, explore,
　look into, search, dig, delve

resemblance　likeness, similarity, sameness

resentment　displeasure, irritation, annoyance,
　vexation, bitterness, wrath, anger,
　indignation

reserve　keep, hold, save, store, preserve, put
　aside

resign　give up, relinquish, surrender, yield,
　waive, forego, renounce, abandon, retire,
　quit, vacate, abdicate

resist　oppose, withstand, counteract　*comply,*
　yield

resolve　determine, decide, settle

resourceful　skilful, clever, deft, adept,
　ingenious, smart, cunning

respect　admire, regard, esteem, appreciate,
　value, revere, honour, idolize, adore

respond　answer, reply, retort, acknowledge,
　react

responsible　1 accountable, answerable, liable
　exempt; 2 trustworthy, reliable, dependable,
　faithful, loyal　*irresponsible, undependable*

rest　1 repose, pause, recess, recline, lounge;
　2 remains, residue, leftovers, balance

restless　uneasy, disturbed, troubled, agitated,
　excited, disquieted, fidgety, impatient,
　anxious　*calm, composed*

restore　put back, replace, reinstate, repair,
　mend, fix, overhaul, renew, renovate

restrain　hold back, keep down, control, check,
　arrest, inhibit, curb, suppress, smother, stifle,
　retard, impede, limit, confine, restrict

restrict　confine, limit, restrain, bound, cramp,
　hamper, impede　*free, liberate*

result consequence, end, effect, outcome,
upshot, fruit, product, conclusion

resume continue, return to, go on with

retain keep, hold, maintain, preserve, save
relinquish

retaliate reciprocate, retort, strike back,
revenge, avenge

retire 1 resign, quit, vacate, relinquish,
abdicate; 2 withdraw, discharge, dismiss,
expel, remove, suspend; 3 retreat, recede;
4 go to bed

retiring shy, modest, reserved, timid, bashful,
restrained, distant *outgoing, aggressive*

retract withdraw, repeal, revoke, rescind,
recall, cancel, annul, invalidate

retreat withdraw, fall back, retire, reverse
advance

retrieve recover, regain, recoup, get back,
reclaim, repossess, retake, salvage, rescue,
redeem, save

return 1 go back, come back, revert, revisit;
2 give back, repay, reimburse

reunion gathering, assembly, meeting,
get-together, social, reception

reveal show, display, open, disclose, expose,
manifest, exhibit, demonstrate, present, bare,
divulge *hide, conceal*

revenge retaliate, get even with

revenue income, earnings, receipts, profits,
returns, proceeds

reverse revert, regress, return, back up
advance

review 1 study, remember, recall, learn;
2 examine, inspect, survey, observe, look at,
consider, criticize, size up

revise correct, change, improve, alter, rewrite,
amend

revive   restore, refresh, bring back, renew, regenerate, resurrect, resuscitate

revoke   repeal, cancel, withdraw, rescind, retract, recall, abolish, annul, invalidate, overrule

revolt   1 rebel, mutiny, rise up, riot, revolutionize *obey*;   2 offend, repel, sicken, nauseate, disgust, horrify, appal *please, delight*

revolution   1 change, revolt, overthrow, rebellion, riot, uprising;   2 circle, circuit, cycle, orbit, turning

revolve   turn, go around, circle

reward   compensate, pay, remunerate, award

rhythm   beat, swing, tempo, metre

rich   1 abounding, fertile, productive, prolific *sterile*;   2 wealthy, affluent, well-to-do, prosperous, opulent, comfortable *poor*;   3 valuable, costly, elegant, priceless, expensive *cheap*;   4 flavourful *tasteless*

rid   clear, free, do away with

riddle   puzzle, enigma, conundrum

ridiculous   nonsensical, foolish, crazy, preposterous, outrageous, bizarre, unbelievable, ludicrous *sensible, believable*

rift   1 split, break, crack, cleft, fracture, fissure, gap, crevice;   2 falling-out, estrangement, difference, parting, breach, alienation, separation

right   1 good, just, lawful, fitting, suitable, proper, valid, sound;   2 correct, true, exact, accurate, perfect, faultless *wrong*

righteous   virtuous, just, proper, good, moral, pure, worthy *immoral, corrupt*

rigid   1 stiff, firm, unbending, unchanging, hard;   2 stubborn, unyielding, adamant, strict, taut, tense *flexible*

rim   edge, border, margin, fringe

ring   1 sound, peal, toll, chime, tinkle, jingle, clamour;   2 circle, band

riot   revolt, rebel, rise up, mutiny, brawl

rip   tear, break, cut

ripe   developed, ready, mature, full-grown
unripe, green

rise   1 get up, stand , *go down*;   2 go up, advance, ascend, mount *descend*;
3 increase, grow, gain *decrease*;
4 originate, begin, start, appear *end*;
5 revolt, rebel, riot, mutiny

risk   chance, hazard, gamble, venture, endanger, imperil, jeopardize, expose

ritual   ceremony, formality, service, exercise, rite

rival   match, compete with, vie with

road   path, track, trail, thoroughfare, lane

roar   thunder, boom, clamour

rob   steal, burgle, loot, sack, pillage, plunder, thieve, pilfer, filch

rock   1 sway, swing, reel, lurch, roll, bob, flounder, tumble, pitch, toss;   2 stone

rogue   rascal, scamp, scoundrel, mischief-maker, imp, elf, pixie, villain

role   capacity, character, part, position, function

roll   turn, move, rotate, pivot, swivel, gyrate, wheel

room   1 space, scope, margin, latitude, leeway;   2 chamber

root   cause, source, origin, derivation

rosy   bright, cheerful, sunny, optimistic, favourable, encouraging

rot   decay, spoil, disintegrate, go bad, crumble

rotate   spin, turn, gyrate, swivel, pivot

rough   1 coarse, unsmooth, bumpy, choppy, shaggy, broken, uneven, irregular *smooth*;
2 harsh, rowdy, severe, fierce, difficult, gruff,

brusque, rude, crude, curt, surly, blunt, tough, snappy   *gentle*

round   circular, globular, rotund, spherical

rouse   stir, excite, arouse, awaken, move, provoke, pique, kindle, inflame, foment, stimulate, agitate, disturb, shake

route   course, circuit, path, rounds, itinerary

routine   habit, method, system, arrangement, order

1. row   1 line, file, string, train, series, sequence, succession, column;   2 paddle

2. row   quarrel, noise, fracas, brawl, dispute, squabble, rumpus

rowdy   rough, disorderly, naughty, bad, misbehaving, boisterous, rumbustious   *well-mannered*

royal   majestic, noble, dignified, stately, grand, regal, imperial, aristocratic

rub   massage, scrub, scour, buff, stroke

rubbish   1 waste, trash, garbage, refuse, scrap, debris, litter, junk;   2 nonsense, silliness, absurdity, poppycock

rude   impolite, rough, coarse, discourteous, uncivil, disrespectful, insolent, ill-mannered, ill-behaved, vulgar, boorish, gruff, brusque, curt, blunt, harsh, surly, impudent, impertinent, saucy, crude, crass, flip, cocky, cheeky   *polite, well-mannered*

rug   carpet, mat, covering

rugged   1 rough, uneven, jagged, ragged, rocky, snaggy   *smooth*;   2 sturdy, vigorous, strong, powerful, potent, stalwart, hardy, robust, muscular, athletic, brawny, well-built, healthy, hale, husky, hefty, beefy   *weak, feeble*

ruin   destroy, spoil, mar, upset, wreck, devastate, ravage, demolish

rule 1 govern, control, reign, dominate, regulate, command, head, lead, direct, manage, supervise, administer, decree, dictate, order, instruct, prevail, guide, influence; 2 measure, mark off

rumble roar, thunder, boom, roll

rumour gossip, broadcast, circulate, spread word

run 1 hasten, hurry, speed, sprint, bound, flee, bolt, race *slow up*; 2 go, move, operate, work; 3 stretch, extend, reach, range, lie, spread; 4 flow, stream, pour, gush, discharge; 5 continue, last, endure, persist *stop*; 6 campaign; 7 conduct, manage, direct, regulate, handle, govern, administer, lead, head, guide, steer, pilot, supervise, oversee, boss; 8 tear, ravel; 9 span, period, time, spell

runway path, track, road

rural countrified, rustic, provincial, bucolic

rush 1 speed, hasten, hurry, dash, dart, scurry, race, run, expedite, accelerate *slow up*; 2 pressure, push, attack, charge, besiege, drive, assult, storm

rusty 1 corroded, eroded, worn, old; 2 unpractised

rut habit, routine

ruthless cruel, merciless, heartless, cold, unfeeling, brutal, savage, inhumane *kind*

S

sack 1 plunder, steal, pillage, loot, rob, fleece; 2 bag, pack

sacred religious, holy, spiritual

sacrifice give up, relinquish, release, surrender, yield, waive, forego, lose, forfeit

sad sorrowful, unhappy, dejected, depressed, blue, melancholy, downcast, discouraged, gloomy, sombre, glum, morose, sullen, grievous, miserable, pathetic, unfortunate, forlorn *happy, glad*

safe secure, unharmed, protected, guarded, sheltered, shielded *endangered, unsafe*

safeguard shield, screen, bulwark, precaution

sail glide, coast, skim, navigate, cruise, float

salary pay, wages, remuneration, compensation

salvage save, rescue, recover, redeem, retrieve *lose*

same identical, alike, equivalent *different*

sample test, experiment, try

sanction permit, approve, allow, authorize, support, license, accept, O.K. *deny*

sanctuary refuge, asylum, haven

sane sensible, sound, rational, logical

sanitary clean, hygienic, sterile, pure, prophylactic, spotless, healthful *dirty, insanitary*

sarcastic sneering, cutting, stinging, bitter, sharp, caustic

satisfy 1 please, gratify, content, benefit, suit, appease *deny*; 2 convince, persuade, assure, comfort, relieve

saucy rude, impudent, impertinent, pert, disrespectful, flippant, cocky, flip, cheeky *polite*

savage uncivilized, barbarous, fierce, cruel, wild, untamed, ruthless, inhumane *civilized, gentle*

save 1 store, economize, scrimp, preserve, conserve, keep, maintain, reserve, accumulate, gather *spend, discard*; 2 rescue, protect, salvage, recover, redeem, retrieve

say 1 speak, declare, recite, utter, voice, express, tell, communicate, remark, comment, mention, assert, relate; 2 power, authority, right, prerogative

scandal disgrace, humiliation, shame, slander

scar blemish, mar, mark, wound, deface

scare frighten, alarm, startle, unnerve, terrify, horrify, appal

scatter disperse, distribute, spread, separate, part, split up, squander, strew *gather, collect*

scene 1 view, picture, sight, vista, lookout, landscape, setting; 2 act; 3 storm, outburst, explosion, flare-up

scent smell, odour, essence, fragrance

schedule list, index, post, enumerate, slate, programme, line-up

scheme plan, plot, intrigue, conspire, connive, contrive

scholar learned person, savant, student

school educate, teach, instruct, enlighten, direct, guide

scope extent, degree, measure, range, sphere, space, reach

score 1 calculate, compute, figure, tally; 2 gain, earn, get, acquire, attain, win; 3 cut, mark, line, scratch, stroke

scornful mocking, disdainful, contemptuous

scramble 1 mix, mingle, blend, combine, jumble, merge, fuse *separate*; 2 hurry, scoot, scurry, scamper, hasten, rush, tear, dart, hustle, scuttle, bustle

scrap 1 fight, quarrel, struggle, squabble, tiff, bicker, row; 2 small amount, shred, snatch, speck, particle; 3 waste, litter, debris, trash, rubbish, junk

scrape 1 rub, brush, skim, graze, grate; 2 trouble, predicament, plight, pinch, strait, mess, complication, muddle, embarrassment

scratch scrape, mark, cut, graze, score, scar, engrave

scream yell, cry, shout, howl, shriek, screech, wail, squall, bawl, shout

screen 1 shelter, protect, hide, cover, cloak, veil, shade, safeguard; 2 sift, strain, filter, refine, sort, separate; 3 inspect, analyze, check

screw fasten, tighten, twist, rotate, turn

scribble scrawl, scratch

scrub scour, clean, polish, wash, rub, buff, massage, shine

scrupulous careful, meticulous, exacting, particular, precise, fussy, fastidious *careless*

scuffle struggle, fight, tussle, mêlée

sculpture carve, form, shape, mould, model, chisel

seal 1 fasten, close, shut, lock *open*; 2 endorse, sign, mark, stamp; 3 sea lion

search seek, look for, hunt, explore

season 1 flavour, spice; 2 time

secluded concealed, hidden, covered, obscured, secret, private, intimate, undisturbed, withdrawn, isolated, remote *accessible, open*

secret hidden, mysterious, private, concealed, secluded *open*

section divide, slice, split, partition, parcel, portion

secure 1 safe, protected, sure, sound, firm, stable *unsafe*; 2 get, obtain, acquire; 3 close, fasten, shut, lock, seal, fix, attach

seduce tempt, persuade, lure, entice, lead on

seek hunt, search, look for, pursue, quest, explore

seem appear, look

seize clutch, grasp, grab, grip, clasp, snatch *release*

seldom rarely, infrequently, hardly, not often *often*

select pick, choose
self-conscious shy, timid, bashful, coy, demure
selfish egotistical, self-centred, possessive
  generous
sell market, vend, peddle *buy*
send dispatch, transmit, forward *receive*
senior elder, older *junior*
sensational exciting, startling, superb,
  exquisite, magnificent, marvellous,
  wonderful, glorious
sense 1 feel, perceive, understand, realize,
  comprehend, fathom, follow, grasp, discern;
  2 intelligence, mentality, judgment
senseless 1 unconscious, lifeless, inanimate,
  oblivious; 2 foolish, stupid, asinine, silly,
  inane, idiotic *bright, sensible*
sensible wise, intelligent, understanding,
  rational, bright, sound, sane, logical,
  practical, realistic *senseless*
sentimental emotional, tender, affectionate
separate divide, part, segregate, sort, isolate,
  partition *join, unite*
sequel continuation, supplement, outcome,
  follow-up
sequence succession, continuation, series,
  progression
serial consecutive, sequential, periodic
serious 1 thoughtful, grave, reflective, pensive,
  solemn, engrossed, sincere, earnest, zealous
  frivolous; 2 important, weighty, momentous,
  profound *minor, unimportant*
serve 1 supply, furnish, deliver, present;
  2 work for, help, assist
set place, position, arrange, fix, adjust,
  regulate
setting scenery, surroundings, background
settle 1 determine, decide, resolve, fix,
  reconcile, mend, patch up; 2 occupy,
  inhabit, colonize, locate

several some, various, assorted, diversified, many, numerous

shabby worn, ragged, shoddy, tattered, frayed, seedy

shaggy rumpled, tousled, dishevelled, long-haired

shake 1 vibrate, tremble, shiver, quiver, quaver, jerk, twitch; 2 jar, bump, bounce, pump, jolt, rock, sway

sham fraud, pretence, fake, mock, imitation, hoax

shambles mess, disorder, chaos

shameful disgraceful, humiliating, scandalous, pitiful, deplorable *righteous*

shape form, fashion, mould, design, develop, adapt

share divide, proportion, apportion, distribute, allot

sharp 1 pointed, angular *dull*; 2 severe, biting, caustic, bitter, harsh, curt, gruff, brusque, blunt *charming*; 3 keen, bright, smart, clever, shrewd, alert, brainy *dull, stupid*

shatter destroy, smash, fragment, break

shed 1 cast, throw off, slough, spread, radiate; 2 hut, shanty, shack

shelter protect, shield, hide, guard, defend, screen, cover, harbour *expose*

shield defend, protect, guard, shelter, hide, screen, cover, cloak, harbour *expose*

shift change, substitute, alter, vary

shifty tricky, sneaky, sly, furtive, deceitful, evasive, crafty, foxy, cunning, artful, shrewd, canny *honest*

shine 1 glow, gleam, glimmer, twinkle, sparkle, glisten, glare; 2 be smart, be bright

ship transport, send, dispatch, haul

shiver shake, quiver, quaver, quake, tremble

shock   startle, frighten, terrify, horrify, appal, awe

shore   coast, beach, waterfront, bank

short   1 little, small, slight, puny   *big*;   2 brief, concise, succinct, curt   *long*

shortage   lack, deficiency, want, need, deficit, absence   *abundance*

shout   yell, call, cry, scream, shriek, howl, clamour

shove   push, jostle, thrust, ram, bump, prod, goad, nudge

show   1 direct, point, aim, explain, clarify, demonstrate, illustrate, indicate, denote, manifest, guide;   2 display, exhibit, reveal   *conceal, hide*

shrewd   keen, clever, sharp, smart, artful, cunning, knowing, crafty, foxy, smooth, canny   *dull, dimwitted*

shriek   yell, cry, call, shout, howl, scream, screech

shrink   1 shrivel, wither, dwindle, become smaller;   2 withdraw, recoil, pull back, retreat, flinch, cringe

shrivel   wither, shrink, wrinkle

shudder   tremble, quiver, shake, quake

shuffle   1 scrape, drag, scuff, trudge;   2 mix, combine, scramble, jumble

shut   close, fasten, seal, lock   *open*

shy   bashful, timid, coy, demure   *aggressive*

sick   ill, ailing, indisposed   *healthy, well*

sight   vision, view, look, vista, scene, spectacle, display, show

sign   1 mark, endorse, seal, initial;   2 signal, gesture, motion, wave, indicate

significance   meaning, connotation, implication, drift, substance, gist, effect, importance, consequence   *unimportance, insignificance*

silent quiet, still, noiseless, soundless, hushed *noisy*

silhouette outline, contour, profile, configuration, shadow

silly foolish, ridiculous, inane, senseless, asinine *sensible*

similar alike, like, resembling, same

simple 1 easy, effortless *difficult*; 2 bare, mere, common, ordinary, sheer, plain; 3 dull, stupid, half-witted, idiotic, moronic, ignorant *bright*

sin wrongdoing, misconduct, crime, vice, offence, evil, error, indiscretion

sincere genuine, real, honest, authentic, legitimate, bona fide, unaffected *insincere, phony*

sing vocalize, chant, croon, hum, serenade

sinister bad, evil, dishonest, wrong, corrupt, fraudulent, crooked *righteous*

sink 1 fall, go down, decline, slump, settle, lower, submerge; 2 weaken, droop, pine, fade

siren alarm, whistle, signal, noisemaker

sit perch, be seated

site place, location, position, situation, whereabouts

situation 1 place, location, position, whereabouts; 2 circumstances, case, condition, terms

size proportion, measure, extent, scope, dimensions

skilful expert, adept, proficient, apt, handy, clever, masterful, able, capable *awkward, unskilful, clumsy*

skinny lean, spare, scrawny, lanky, gaunt, bony *chubby*

skip 1 spring, jump, leap; 2 pass over, omit, bypass *include*

skirmish argument, conflict, clash, scuffle, brush, struggle, encounter, engagement, mêlée, fracas, brawl, dog-fight, rumpus

slack 1 loose, lax, baggy, hanging, droopy *tight*; 2 slow, dull, lazy, inactive *busy*

slam close, bang, shut

slander libel, slur, discredit, smear

slap hit, smack, crack

slaughter butchery, massacre, killing, carnage, genocide

slavery bondage, servitude, serfdom *freedom*

sleek smooth, glossy, slick, polished

sleep slumber, doze, drowse, nap, rest, snooze

slender thin, narrow, svelte, frail, slight *stout*

slice cut, sever, split, carve, slash, slit

slick 1 sleek, smooth, glossy, polished; 2 sly, tricky, cunning, shrewd, shifty, crafty, foxy

slide glide, coast, skim, skid, slip

slight 1 small, petite, puny, tiny *large, gross*; 2 slender, frail, delicate, dainty, flimsy, thin *stout*; 3 neglect, disregard, overlook, ignore

slim slender, thin, slight, lean *stout*

sling 1 throw, cast, hurl, fling, pitch, toss, heave, flip; 2 suspend, hang; 3 bandage, support, splint

slip 1 slide, glide, skid; 2 mistake, error, oversight, blunder

slit cut, sever, split, cleave, tear

slogan motto, phrase, expression, cry

slope slant, incline, tip, lean, tilt

sloppy 1 careless, slovenly, slipshod, negligent, haphazard, messy *neat*; 2 wet, slushy *dry*

slovenly untidy, slipshod, unkempt, shabby, seedy, messy, sloppy *neat*

slow 1 lingering, delaying, lackadaisical, leisurely, poking, tarrying, dillydallying *fast*; 2 dull, stupid *quick, bright*

sluggish slow-moving, inactive, lackadaisical, poky, listless, lethargic *quick, fast-moving*

sly shrewd, underhanded, artful, cunning, shifty, smooth, crafty, canny, sneaky, clever, tricky

smack 1 hit, slap, crack, strike, whack; 2 kiss

small 1 little, slight, puny, insignificant *big*; 2 unimportant, trivial *important*

smart 1 bright, clever, keen, intelligent, quick, shrewd, alert, brainy *stupid*; 2 stylish, well-dressed, chic, natty, dapper, fashionable; 3 pain, ache, hurt

smash 1 destroy, shatter, ruin, break, crash, fragment; 2 collide, clash, bump, strike, knock, bang

smear 1 strain, mark, soil, tarnish, smudge, spot; 2 spoil, harm, blacken, defile, slander

smell scent, odour, essence, fragrance

smile grin, beam, laugh, smirk *frown*

smooth 1 sleek, slick, glossy, polished, even, level *rough*; 2 polite, pleasant, suave, chivalrous, cunning

smother suffocate, stifle, choke, asphyxiate, muffle, suppress

smudge smear, mark, soil, blacken, spot, stain

smug self-satisfied, confident, vain, conceited, arrogant, boastful, egotistical *modest, humble*

snap 1 break, burst, split, crack; 2 snatch, seize *release*

snatch 1 seize, grasp, grab, clutch, hook, snag, snare, trap release; 2 small amount, bit, scrap, shred

sneak lurk, prowl, slink, steal, creep

sneer mock, scoff, jeer, taunt

sniff smell, scent, inhale

snobbish haughty, arrogant, priggish

snoop pry, meddle, intrude, interfere

snooze sleep, doze, nap

snub slight, ignore, avoid, shun, spurn, rebuff

snug 1 comfortable, warm, sheltered, cozy, homelike; 2 compact, close, tight *roomy*

soak wet, drench, saturate, steep, sop *dry*

sob cry, weep, bawl, blubber, snivel, wail, howl

sober 1 sensible, calm, moderate, temperate, mild, sound, reasonable *extreme*; 2 unintoxicated, uninebriated *drunk*

sociable friendly, amiable, congenial, cordial, gregarious *unfriendly, unsociable*

society 1 people, folks, public, populace, community, world; 2 company, organization, association, alliance, league, union, federation, sect

soft 1 delicate, tender, flexible, pliable, elastic *hard*; 2 mild, kind, gentle, tender, pleasant, lenient, easygoing *harsh*

soggy damp, soaked, saturated, sopping, waterlogged *dry*

soil 1 dirty, spot, stain, smudge, smear *clean*; 2 slander, libel, defile; 3 ground, earth, dirt, land

sole only, single, one, individual, unique

solemn serious, grave, gloomy, dismal, sombre, dreary, glum *happy, cheerful*

solicit request, appeal, ask, canvass, beg

solid 1 hard, firm, rigid, substantial, sturdy, strong, durable *flimsy, soft*; 2 whole, entire, continuous, complete

solitary single, individual, lone, isolated, unaccompanied

solution 1 explanation, answer, resolution, finding, outcome, result; 2 mixture

solve answer, explain, clear up, work out, figure out, unriddle, decipher, decode

soon promptly, quickly, shortly, presently, directly, before long

soothe   calm, comfort, quiet, ease, pacify, relieve

sordid   dirty, filthy, slovenly, squalid

sore   1 painful, aching, tender, smarting, raw, irritated, inflamed, festering, rankling, throbbing, distressing *healed*;   2 angry, offended, irate, indignant

sorrow   grief, sadness, regret, trouble, misfortune, suffering, woe, anguish, misery, agony, remorse *happiness*

sorry   1 regretful, remorseful, repentant, apologetic;   2 sad, sympathetic, unhappy, miserable, displeased;   3 wretched, poor, pitiful

sort   arrange, separate, classify, categorize, group, divide, catalogue

sound   1 make noise, utter, pronounce, voice;   2 healthy, wholesome, hearty *unhealthy*;   3 strong, safe, secure, stable, substantial, firm, solid, solvent *weak*;   4 correct, right, reasonable, sensible, sane, logical, rational *wrong, foolish*

sour   1 spoiled, fermented, bitter, rancid *fresh*;   2 disagreeable, peevish, unpleasant *pleasant*

source   origin, beginning, derivation, root

souvenir   remembrance, keepsake, memento, relic, token

sovereign   supreme, greatest, regal, royal, imperial, majestic, ruling, reigning, governing

1. sow   scatter, spread, disperse, distribute

2. sow   female pig

space   extent, expanse, measure, dimension, area

spacious   vast, roomy, widespread, extensive, sweeping, far-reaching, capacious *confining, narrow*

spare 1 give up, relinquish, dispense with, do without, omit, forego, part with, sacrifice, surrender, yield *keep*; 2 extra, surplus, remainder, balance, leftover, excess; 3 lean, skinny, thin, scrawny, lanky, bony *stout*

sparkle shine, glitter, flash, glimmer, shimmer, twinkle, glisten

spasm twitch, seizure, convulsion, fit

speak talk, say, tell, express

special unusual, exceptional, particular, extraordinary, notable *ordinary, usual*

species group, class, kind, sort, type, variety

specific definite, precise, particular, special, fixed

specimen sample, representative, type, example

speck tiny bit, particle, iota

spectacle sight, show, display, exhibition, pageant

spectacular dramatic, sensational

speculate 1 guess, theorize, conjecture; 2 gamble, risk, chance, venture; 3 reflect, meditate, consider, contemplate, study, deliberate

speedy fast, rapid, quick, swift, hasty, fleet, expeditious

spell 1 magic power, charm, fascination, trance; 2 time, stretch, shift, period

spellbound fascinated, enchanted, interested, rapt, enthralled, gripped, engrossed, absorbed, awed, charmed, hypnotized, mesmerized *bored*

spend pay out, lay out, use, consume, finish off, exhaust, expend

spill overflow, run over, brim over, cascade, flood, pour

spin turn, twirl, twist, rotate, pivot, wheel, reel, swirl

spirit 1 soul, heart, mind; 2 nature, disposition, temper; 3 courage, vigour, life, vivacity

spiritual religious, sacred, holy

spiteful annoying, malicious, hostile, vindictive, mean

splendid fine, excellent, brilliant, glorious, magnificent, grand

splendour pomp, glory, magnificence, grandeur, brilliance, brightness, radiance *dullness*

split separate, divide, bisect, halve, cleave, partition, sever, break, crack *join, connect*

spoil damage, injure, destroy, botch, impair, mar, ruin, upset, rot, decay

sponsor underwriter, backer, financer, promoter, supporter

spontaneous instinctive, inherent, natural, automatic *planned*

spot 1 stain, mark, discolour, soil; 2 pick out, recognize, know, tell, distinguish, identify, place, discern, spy, sight

sprawl spread, extend, stretch out, expand, fan out

spread 1 stretch out, unfold, extend, sprawl; 2 distribute, scatter, disperse

sprightly lively, gay, active, animated, spirited, vivacious, spry, energetic, nimble *dull, lethargic*

spring leap, jump, bounce, vault, hop, bound, hurdle

sprout grow, develop, shoot up, flourish, thrive, bud, burgeon

spy see, detect, view, observe, discern, sight, spot

squabble quarrel, disagree, differ, dispute, fight, tiff, bicker, row

squad group, unit, company, band, gang, crew, outfit, troop, body

squalid filthy, degraded, poor, wretched,
  shabby, sordid, slummy *clean*

square 1 adjust, settle, balance, equalize;
  2 just, fair, honest, straight, equitable
  crooked; 3 old-fashioned, corny, unaware,
  conventional *sophisticated*

squash crush, press, mash, suppress, squelch

squeal 1 cry, squeak, screech, yell; 2 tattle,
  inform on

squeeze press, crush, pinch, cram

squirt spew, spout, spurt, expel, pour forth, jet,
  gush, spray, surge, splash

stab pierce, perforate, puncture, impale, wound

stable 1 steady, firm, unchanging, steadfast,
  sound, secure, settled, established *unsettled*;
  2 loose-box

staff 1 group, committee, personnel, force,
  crew, gang; 2 stick, pole, rod, sceptre

stage 1 arrange, dramatize, present, produce,
  perform, enact, put on; 2 period, interval,
  point, time, spell; 3 tier, level, layer, story;
  4 platform, podium, rostrum

stagger sway, reel, waver, flounder, tumble,
  lurch

stain spot, soil, mark, discolour

stake 1 bet, wager, gamble, risk; 2 peg, post

stale old, worn, obsolete, musty *new, fresh*

stalk 1 pursue, hunt, chase, seek, search;
  2 stem

stammer stutter, falter, stumble

stamp 1 mark, seal, label, brand, engrave,
  print; 2 trample, pound, crush, tread

stand 1 rise, get up *sit, lie down*; 2 ensure,
  bear, tolerate; 3 remain, last, continue, stay,
  persist; 4 pedestal, base, table

standard 1 model, rule, pattern, criterion,
  ideal; 2 flag, banner, pennant, emblem,
  symbol, colours

stare gaze, look, gape, glare, gawp

stark complete, entirely, downright, absolute, outright

start 1 begin, commence, set out; 2 move suddenly, jerk, jump

startle frighten, surprise, shock, electrify, upset, alarm, unnerve

starve hunger, crave food

state 1 tell, express, say, pose, declare, assert, relate, recite, report, expound; 2 condition, position, status, situation, circumstance; 3 nation

stately grand, majestic, dignified, imposing, noble, grandiose, magnificent, splendid, impressive

statement account, report, announcement, proclamation, declaration, notice

static 1 still, inactive, sluggish, inert, dormant *active*; 2 electrical interference

station 1 place, post; 2 position, rank, standing, status, post

stationary fixed, immovable, immobile, firm, inflexible, motionless *movable*

stationery paper, writing materials

statue figure, sculpture, bust, monument

status 1 standing, position, station, class, division, grade, rank; 2 condition, state

stay 1 remain, last, endure, continue, persist *leave*; 2 dwell, reside, live, occupy, inhabit; 3 delay, detain, retard, stop, hold up *proceed*

steady constant, fixed, inert, regular, incessant, ceaseless, perpetual *changing*

steal rob, take, thieve, pilfer, filch

stealthy secret, sly, sneaky, underhanded, shifty *open, honest*

steam 1 vapour, gas, smoke; 2 power, energy, force; 3 cook, soften, freshen

steep 1 soak, drench, sop, saturate, bathe; 2 high, precipitous

steer 1 guide, direct, drive, manage, regulate, conduct, handle, lead, head, run; 2 cattle

step walk, tread, pace

sterilize clean, sanitize, disinfect, decontaminate

stern severe, strict, harsh, firm, hard, exacting, austere, stringent *lenient, easygoing*

stew 1 cook; 2 fume, seethe, be angry, rage, rave, rant, storm, fret

stick 1 pierce, stab, perforate, penetrate, puncture; 2 fasten, attach, adhere, cling; 3 continue, keep on, persevere *stop, discontinue*

stiff 1 rigid, firm, tense, taut, tight, inflexible, tough *flexible*; 2 formal, unnatural, stilted *informal*; 3 hard, difficult, tough *easy*

stifle smother, stop, suppress, suffocate, choke

still 1 quiet, motionless, noiseless, calm, tranquil, peaceful, placid, smooth, untroubled *noisy*; 2 yet, even, until now, so far

stimulate spur, stir, rouse, energize, invigorate, pep up, activate, motivate, move *suppress, stifle*

sting prick, wound, pain, distress, inflame

stingy ungenerous, miserly, cheap, closefisted *generous, liberal*

stink smell, stench, odour

stint task, work, job, chore, duty, assignment, function, role

stir 1 mix, blend, mingle, combine, merge, scramble, jumble; 2 move, budge, mobilize; 3 excite, affect, agitate, disturb, shake, perturb, trouble, disquiet, rouse

stock supply, keep, store up, collect, accumulate, amass, stockpile, gather, hoard

stomach 1 bear, endure, take stand, tolerate;
2 belly, abdomen

stop end, halt, check, stay, cease, block,
discontinue, quit, arrest, prevent, conclude,
terminate *start*

store 1 supply, stock, keep, collect, accumulate,
amass, stockpile, gather, hoard; 2 shop,
mart, business

storm 1 attack, besiege, beset, raid, charge,
assault, assail; 2 rage, be violent, rant, rave,
rampage, seethe, boil, fume; 3 tempest,
outburst

story 1 tale, account, chronicle, yarn,
narrative, anecdote, epic, saga; 2 floor,
level, tier

stout 1 fat, large, fleshy, plump, pudgy, chubby,
stocky, portly *thin*; 2 brave, bold,
courageous, valiant, gallant, heroic,
chivalrous *meek, cowardly*

stow pack, load, store

straight 1 direct, unswerving *crooked*;
2 frank, honest, upright, square, sincere, open

strain 1 stretch, pull, extend, tug, tow;
2 sprain, wrench, injure, hurt; 3 quality,
trace, streak; 4 race, descent

strange unusual, queer, peculiar, unfamiliar,
odd, curious, eccentric *ordinary, familiar*

strangle choke, suffocate, smother, asphyxiate

strategy planning, management, tactics,
manipulation, intrigue, manoeuvring

streak 1 mark, line, score, striate, stripe;
2 strain, element, vein, nature, quality,
characteristic, tendency

stream 1 flow, pour, surge, rush, gush, flood;
2 creek, brook

street road, thoroughfare, avenue

strength power, force, vigour, potency, might,
energy *weakness*

strenuous 1 active, energetic, vigorous, intense *inactive*; 2 difficult, hard, rough, rugged, arduous, laborious *easy*

stress 1 force, strain, pressure, tension; 2 emphasis, importance, accent, insistence, urgency

stretch extend, draw out, spread, strain, expand, distend, elongate

strict 1 harsh, exact, precise, rigorous, severe, exacting, stringent, stern, austere *lenient*; 2 perfect, complete, absolute, literal, exact, real, true

strike 1 hit, knock, job, smack, whack, bat, clout; 2 revolt, rebel

striking attractive, noticeable, obvious, conspicuous, prominent, bold, pronounced, outstanding, flagrant, glaring *unattractive*

strip remove, uncover, bare, peel, pare *cover*

stroke 1 rub, caress, massage, pet; 2 feat, effort, act, deed, undertaking, attempt; 3 attack, seizure, convulsion, spasm

stroll walk, saunter, stride, strut, amble, promenade

strong powerful, vigorous, forceful, potent, mighty, sturdy, hardy, muscular, brawny *weak*

stronghold fortification, bastion

structure 1 building, construction, house, edifice; 2 form, shape, figure, configuration

struggle 1 endeavour, strive, attempt, try; 2 fight, battle, contend, tussle, scuffle

stubborn obstinate, wilful, headstrong, adamant, rigid, unyielding, inflexible *yielding, flexible*

studious learned, bookish, educated, scholarly, cultured, profound, erudite, diligent

stuff 1 fill, load, pack, gorge, saturate *empty*; 2 substance, matter, material

stuffy 1 close, stifling, airless, suffocating, oppressive *airy*; 2 pompous, prim, prudish, strait-laced, unimaginative, dull, staid, stodgy, old-fogyish *casual, regular*

stunning 1 attractive, good-looking, beautiful, gorgeous, ravishing, glorious, dazzling, brilliant *unattractive*; 2 bewildering, astounding, shocking, astonishing, amazing, surprising

stunt 1 shorten, abbreviate, abridge, condense; 2 feat, act, exploit, performance

stupendous amazing, marvellous, great, huge, enormous, immense, vast, extraordinary, exceptional, remarkable, wonderful

stupid dull, unintelligent, dense, asinine, silly, foolish *smart, bright*

sturdy strong, firm, powerful, rugged, hardy, robust, vigorous, well-built, athletic, muscular, brawny, sound, stable, substantial, solid, durable *weak, shaky*

stutter stammer, hem, falter, hesitate

stylish fashionable, modish, voguish, smart, chic, well-dressed, natty, dapper, sporty *drab*

subdue conquer, overcome, crush, vanquish, suppress, quell, put down, squash

subject topic, issue, problem, theme, text, question, point, plot

submit yield, surrender, comply, obey, heed, mind

subordinate dependent, secondary, inferior *superior*

subscribe contribute, give to, donate to, support

subsequent following, later, coming after, succeeding, next *preceding*

subside decrease, diminish, lessen, decline *increase*

substance matter, material, body, stuff, essence, gist, content

substantial 1 real, actual, true, authentic *vague*; 2 strong, firm, solid, stable, sound *weak*; 3 wealthy, well-to-do, rich, affluent, prosperous *poor*

substitute replace, change, exchange, switch, shift

subtle 1 delicate, thin, fine, faint *gross, strong*; 2 sly, crafty, tricky, underhand, shrewd, cunning, foxy, clever *open, honest*

successful prosperous, fortunate, well-off, thriving, flourishing, victorious, triumphant, winning, providential, booming, lucky *failing, unsuccessful*

succession sequence, order, progression, series

succumb 1 yield, give way, submit, comply, acquiesce *conquer*; 2 die, decease, expire, perish

suck drink, take it, absorb, draw in

sudden unexpected, abrupt, hasty, unforeseen, impulsive, impetuous *planned, deliberate*

sue prosecute, bring action against, litigate

suffer endure, experience, bear, stand, tolerate, undergo

sufficient enough, ample, plenty, satisfactory, adequate *lacking, insufficient*

suffocate smother, stifle, choke, muffle, suppress, asphyxiate

suffrage vote, voice, ballot

suggest hint, imply, intimate, insinuate, propose, advise

suit 1 agree with, satisfy; 2 fit, become; 3 costume, dress, habit; 4 legal action, litigation, case, prosecution

suitable fitting, proper, timely, favourable, adequate, satisfactory *unsuitable*

sum total, whole, entirety, quantity, amount

summarize outline, abridge, encapsulate, précis *expand, elaborate*

summit top, peak, crest, crown, apex, acme, zenith *bottom, base*

summon call, send for, subpoena, conjure

sumptuous rich, magnificent, costly, grandiose, grand, splendid, imposing, impressive, stately, majestic, elegant, elaborate, luxurious *poor*

sunken 1 submerged, sunk; 2 hollow, concave

sunny bright, cheerful, pleasant, radiant *dull*

superb grand, stately, magnificent, splendid, fine, excellent, exquisite, marvellous, wonderful, grandiose, glorious, imposing, impressive, noble, majestic, sumptuous, elaborate *inferior*

superficial shallow, surface, cursory *thorough, deep*

superior better, greater, higher *inferior*

supernatural spiritual, superhuman, ghostly, unknown, mysterious, mystical

superstition folklore, tradition, popular belief, old wives' tale

supervise direct, oversee, govern, regulate, command, head, lead, administer, boss

supple bending, pliable, flexible, plastic, elastic, yielding, limber, lithe *stiff, firm*

supplement add to, complete, augment, increase, fortify, reinforce *subtract*

supply furnish, provide, stock, store

support help, aid, bolster, sustain, defend, encourage, foster

suppose believe, think, imagine, consider, assume, infer, deduce, presume

suppress restrain, repress, keep down, hold back, inhibit, curb, check, arrest, bridle, squelch, stifle, subdue, squash, restrict, limit, quell *foster, encourage*

supreme   highest, greatest, utmost, extreme, uppermost, top, maximum, foremost, chief, paramount

sure   certain, positive, absolute, definite, decided

surface   outside, exterior, face   *interior*

surplus   excess, extra, superfluous, remaining, leftover, spare, additional, supplementary   *lack*

surprise   astonish, amaze, catch unaware, astound, bewilder, awe, dumbfound

surrender   give up, yield, relinquish, forego, renounce, submit, capitulate, abandon   *conquer*

surround   wrap, envelop, embrace, encircle, enclose, encompass

survey   1 examine, view, inspect, scrutinize, observe, scan, study, contemplate, peruse, review;   2 measure, gauge, assess, estimate, rate, appraise

survive   remain, continue, outlast, outlive

suspect   1 think, guess, suppose, assume, imagine, surmise, infer, gather;   2 doubt, distrust, question, challenge, dispute, mistrust   *trust*

suspend   1 hang, sling;   2 postpone, delay, defer, hold over, shelve;   3 interrupt, break, arrest, halt   *continue*

suspense   anxiety, fear, concern, apprehension, distress, uneasiness, agitation, disquiet

suspicious   suspecting, doubtful, questionable, wary

sustain   keep up, support, bear, endure, maintain, suffer, tolerate, stand, abide   *succumb*

swallow   1 eat, absorb, consume, devour, gulp, ingest;   2 accept, take, believe

swap   trade, deal, exchange, barter, switch

swarm crowd, throng, collect, assemble, meet, gather, cluster *disperse, scatter*

swear 1 promise, vow, vouch; 2 curse

sweet 1 sugary, saccharine *bitter*; 2 pleasant, agreeable, lovely, charming, adorable *unpleasant*

swell 1 grow bigger, increase, gain, expand, enlarge, broaden, amplify, magnify, inflate, stretch, bulge, billow *shrink, decrease*

swerve dodge, sidestep, shift, turn

swift fast, quick, rapid, speedy, hasty, fleet, expeditious, agile, nimble *slow*

swindle cheat, defraud, fleece

swing sway, reel, rock, roll, lurch, fluctuate, dangle, hang

switch 1 whip, strike, slash, beat, thrash, bang, spank, flog, pummel, lash, strap, club, paddle; 2 change, turn, shift, exchange, substitute, replace, trade, swap

symbolize represent, stand for, typify, illustrate

sympathy understanding, tolerance, sensitivity, pity, compassion, mercy, commiseration, condolence

symptom sign, implication, token, mark, omen, indication

system plan, scheme, method, design, arrangement, order

T

table list, chart, index, catalogue, schedule

tackle 1 undertake, get busy, attack; 2 seize, grapple with; 3 equipment, apparatus, gear, furnishings

tact grace, diplomacy, taste, finesse, sensitivity, sensibility

tactics procedures, operations, methods, strategy, manoeuvre

take 1 seize, capture, get, receive, gain, obtain, procure *give*; 2 need, require, involve, entail, implicate; 3 choose, select, pick out; 4 bring, carry, convey; 5 suppose, assume, infer, understand, gather, guess; 6 hire, lease, engage; 7 tolerate, endure, bear, stand, suffer, swallow, stomach

tale 1 story, yarn, account, narrative, epic, saga; 2 falsehood, lie, untruth, fib *truth*

talent ability, skill, gift, endowment, genius, capability, capacity, forte, aptitude

talk 1 speak, converse, discuss; 2 gossip, rumour, report

tall 1 high, big, long, lengthy *short*; 2 exaggerated, magnified, enlarged, overstated, excessive, extreme *true*

tally 1 count, score, calculate, compute, estimate, reckon, figure, list; 2 agree, correspond, coincide, match, check

tame gentle, obedient, temperate, mild, domesticated *wild*

tangible 1 real, actual, definite, substantial, concrete *vague*; 2 touchable

tangle twist, confuse, mess, complicate, knot, snarl, involve

target object, goal, aim, end, mark, point

task work, duty, job, chore, stint, assignment, function

taste savour, sample, experiment, test, try, experience, sense, feel

tax 1 strain, burden, load, encumber, oppress; 2 duty, tariff, levy, toll, assessment

teach instruct, educate, show, enlighten, tutor, coach, direct, guide

team band, company, group, party, gang, crew

tear cut, sever, split, slash, slice, slit, rip

tease annoy, vex, pester, bother, joke, jest, banter, badger

tedious dull, dreary, slow, dry, tiring, boring, monotonous, humdrum, wearisome *exhilarating, interesting*

tell say, inform, utter, voice, express, communicate, convey, impart, state, declare, assert, relate, recite, remark, comment, note, mention

temper disposition, condition, nature, character, constitution, tendency, mood

temperamental moody, sensitive, touchy, thin-skinned

temperate moderate, mild, gentle, calm *extreme*

temporary passing, momentary, transient, short-lived *lasting, permanent*

tempt invite, attract, interest, appeal, tantalize, titillate, entice, seduce, lure

tenant dweller, occupant, resident, inhabitant

tend 1 be apt, be likely, incline, lean; 2 attend, administer, care for, look after, mind, watch over, foster, nurse, serve, help

tendency inclination, leaning, bent, proclivity, disposition, aptitude

tender 1 soft, delicate, gentle, kind, affectionate, loving, sensitive *harsh, rough*; 2 offer, present, submit, extend

tense strained, stretched, tight, rigid, taut *relaxed*

term 1 period, time, duration; 2 condition, premise; 3 name, call, designate, dub, title, label, tag

terminate end, finish, close, conclude, stop, cease, complete *begin*

terrible dreadful, horrible, deplorable, outrageous, scandalous, vile, wretched, abominable, detestable, despicable,

contemptible, shocking, appalling
wonderful, superb
terrific great, superb, magnificent, marvellous,
wonderful, colossal, tremendous, glorious,
divine, sensational
terrify frighten, horrify, appal, shock, awe,
petrify, paralyze, stupefy
territory land, region, area, zone, place,
country, district, section
test 1 examine, question, quiz, interrogate,
query, grill, cross-examine; 2 experiment,
try, prove, verify
testimony evidence, proof, statement,
declaration
text subject, topic, theme, issue, point,
question, problem, thesis, proposition
texture structure, construction, composition,
make-up, finish, grain
thankful grateful, appreciative, obliged,
indebted *thankless*
theme 1 subject, topic, text, question, problem,
issue, point, proposition; 2 composition,
paper, article, treatise, essay, dissertation,
discourse, discussion, study, thesis; 3 motif
theory explanation, speculation, supposition,
hypothesis, inference, opinion, impression,
idea, thought, attitude, view, conception,
judgment
therefore hence, consequently, accordingly,
for that reason
thick 1 broad, massive, bulky, coarse
narrow; 2 numerous, swarming, teeming,
crowded *empty*; 3 stupid, dense, asinine,
dull *bright*
thief robber, pilferer, filcher, burglar, crook
thin 1 slender, lean, slim, slight, frail, skinny,
gaunt, lanky *fat*; 2 scanty, sparse,
meagre *plentiful*

think 1 believe, expect, imagine, deem, fancy, presume, gather, deduce, judge, conclude, guess, suppose, assume, suspect, infer, understand; 2 consider, contemplate, reflect, study, ponder, deliberate, meditate, reason, concentrate, muse, theorize

thirsty 1 dry, arid, parched, dehydrated; 2 desirous, craving, hungering for *satisfied*

thorough complete, intensive, sweeping, all-out, full *shallow, incomplete*

thoroughfare passage, road, highway, street, avenue, boulevard, turnpike

though however, in any case, nevertheless, notwithstanding

thought 1 thinking, idea, notion, contemplation, reflection, consideration, reasoning, deliberation, meditation; 2 care, attention, regard, concern, indulgence *thoughtlessness*

threaten 1 warn, caution, advise, admonish, alert, forebode; 2 menace, intimidate, bully, terrorize, harrass, browbeat, bulldoze

thrifty economical, saving, frugal, prudent, careful, economizing, sparing *wasteful*

thrill tingle, excite, titillate, delight, enrapture, enthrall, enchant, charm *bore*

thrive prosper, grow, develop, increase, sprout, flourish, mushroom, boom, bloom *shrivel, fade, fail*

throb beat, pulsate, palpitate, pound, thump

throw toss, cast, furl, fling, pitch, heave, chuck, flip, sling

thus therefore, hence, consequently, accordingly, so

tickle amuse, delight, titillate, entertain, charm, thrill, excite

tidy 1 neat, orderly, trim, well-kept, shipshape *sloppy*; 2 considerable, large, sizable, grand, big, goodly, substantial

tie   fasten, bind, lash, wrap, strap   *untie, open*

tight   1 firm, rigid, stiff, taut, tense   *relaxed*;
2 snug, compact, close   *loose*;   3 scarce, hard
to get, sparse, rare, skimpy   *plentiful*;
4 stingy, ungenerous, closefisted, miserly
generous

till   1 cultivate, plough, work;   2 money drawer,
cash register, moneybox, vault, safe,
depository

tilt   tip, slope, slant, incline, lean, list

time   1 duration, period, interval, spell, term,
age, generation, era, epoch;   2 occasion,
opportunity, chance, opening;   3 rhythm,
tempo, metre, measure

timetable   schedule, list, programme

timid   shy, bashful, coy, demure, reserved,
restrained, retiring, meek, sheepish, fearful,
cowardly, shrinking   *bold*

tinge   colour, tint, stain, dye

tint   colour, tinge, dye, stain, shade

tiny   small, minute, undersized, little, slight,
puny, wee   *large*

tip   1 end, extremity, limit, tail, point;   2 slope,
slant, tilt, list, leaning, inclination;
3 gratuity, premium, bonus;   4 advice,
warning, information, pointer

tired   weary, exhausted, fatigued, weak, run-
down   *rested*

title   name, label, tag, designation, caption,
headline

together   collectively, simultaneously,
concurrently, jointly, cooperatively   *alone*

token   1 proof, sign, indication, evidence, clue,
mark, symptom;   2 memento, remembrance,
trophy, souvenir, keepsake, relic;   3 ticket,
certificate, voucher, coupon, check

tolerate   allow, permit, bear, endure, suffer,
stand, abide, accept   *prohibit, forbid*

tomb grave, vault, crypt, shrine, mausoleum

tone 1 sound, pitch, key, note, intonation;
2 spirit, character, style, nature, quality,
mood; 3 condition, vigour, shape; 4 colour,
shade, hue, tint, tinge, stain, complexion

too 1 also, besides, additionally, as well,
furthermore; 2 very, exceedingly,
excessively

tool implement, instrument, utensil, apparatus,
device, gadget, appliance

top head, highest, summit, peak, crown, tip,
apex, acme, zenith, maximum *bottom, tail,
toe*

topic subject, theme, text, question, problem,
issue, point, plot

torrent flood, burst, eruption, stream,
outbreak, deluge

torture pain, distress, torment, agonize,
harrow, inflame, persecute, plague

toss throw, cast, fling, pitch, hurl, sling, heave,
chuck, flip

total 1 whole, entire, complete *partial*;
2 add, sum up, figure up, count

touch 1 feel, contact, finger, handle,
manipulate; 2 graze, brush, reach, scrape,
skim; 3 affect, move, stir, impress, strike;
4 borrow, ask for, beg

touching tender, provoking, affecting, moving,
pathetic

tough 1 hardy, strong, firm, sturdy, durable
weak; 2 hard, difficult, complicated, obscure,
unclear, vague *easy*

tour journey, travel, voyage

tournament contest, tourney, game, sport,
play

tow pull, heave, haul, tug, draw, drag

towering huge, lofty, high, elevated, soaring,
immense, monumental, gigantic

town metropolis, city, municipality

toxic poisonous, venomous, noxious, deadly, malignant

trace 1 copy, reproduce, duplicate, transcribe, draw, sketch, outline, delineate; 2 seek, track, trail, follow, smell out; 3 bit, small amount, touch, dash

track 1 path, trail, road; 2 mark, trace, sign, clue, evidence

trade 1 exchange, barter, bargain, deal, switch, reciprocate, traffic, swap; 2 vocation, occupation, business, work, line, calling, profession, practice, pursuit, career, craft

tradition custom, long usage, folklore

traffic 1 buy or sell, exchange, trade, bargain, barter, deal; 2 vehicle movement

tragic disastrous, dreadful, sad, catastrophic, grievous

trail 1 follow, pursue, go after, shadow, heel, tail, tag along; 2 track, hunt, trace, run down; 3 path, road, line

train 1 teach, rear, bring up, direct, drill, exercise, practise, prepare, condition, cultivate, discipline, nurture, foster, educate, groom; 2 series, succession, line, sequence, file, string, row, procession, column

traitor betrayer, informer, tattler, blab, spy, undercover man

tramp 1 march, parade, hike; 2 vagabond, vagrant, hobo

trance spell, ecstasy, rapture, hypnosis

tranquil calm, peaceful, quiet, serene, untroubled *noisy, tumultuous*

transfer hand over, deliver, pass, sign over, change hands

transform change, convert, alter

transition change, conversion, transformation, transfer

translate interpret

transmit send over, pass along, dispatch, forward, transfer

transplant transfer, transpose, shift, change, move, reset

trap catch, snare, hook

travel journey, go, proceed, move, pass, progress, traverse

treacherous deceiving, unreliable, two-faced, fraudulent, shifty, tricky, underhand, insidious, shady

treason betrayal, double-dealing

treasure 1 cherish, value highly, hold dear, adore, idolize, worship, prize, appreciate; 2 store, assets, accumulation, collection, funds, resources, abundance, fortune, wealth

treat 1 deal with, think of, consider, regard, handle, behave toward; 2 doctor, minister to, attend, nurse; 3 delight, pleasure, thrill, enjoyment

treaty agreement, compact, alliance, settlement, arrangement, truce, armistice

trek travel, journey, voyage, migration

tremble shake, quake, vibrate, shiver, quiver, quaver, shudder

tremendous 1 enormous, great, huge, immense, vast, titanic, colossal, gigantic, giant *small, minute*; 2 superb, exquisite, magnificent, marvellous, glorious, divine, terrific, sensational *awful*

trend direction, course, tendency, drift, current, movement

trespass intrude, transgress, encroach, infringe, overstep

trial 1 test, experiment, tryout; 2 trouble, hardship, tribulation, ordeal; 3 court case

tribe group, class, set, kind, people, family, sect, breed, clan, folk, culture

tribunal court, forum, board, council

trick deceive, cheat, hoax, dupe, delude,
betray, fool, hoodwink

trickle leak, drip, dribble, drop

tried tested, proved

trigger begin, start, touch off, spark, fire,
kindle *conclude*

trim 1 cut, shave, pare, reduce, lower;
2 decorate, ornament, adorn, dress, garnish,
deck, beautify, embellish, furbish, tidy,
straighten up, clean, fix up, spruce up

trip 1 stumble, tumble, topple, fall; 2 journey,
voyage, trek, tour, expedition, pilgrimage,
excursion, jaunt, junket, outing

triumph victory, success, conquest, winning
defeat

trivial unimportant, petty, trifling, slight,
superficial, shallow, frivolous, light, foolish,
silly, inane *important*

troop group, band, unit, company, party, gang,
crew, body, bunch, crowd, mob

trouble distress, worry, disturb, agitate,
perturb, disquiet, stir, bother, upset,
discomfort, vex, plague *calm, soothe*

truant absentee

truce pause, rest, respite, break, recess,
intermission, interruption, interval,
armistice, peace

true real, actual, unmistaken, veritable,
certain, valid, genuine, authentic, natural,
legitimate, bona fide, right, proper, correct,
exact, accurate *false*

trust believe, credit, accept, rely on, depend
on *distrust*

try 1 attempt, test, experiment, prove, verify,
essay, undertake; 2 judge, prosecute, hear

trying annoying, distressing, difficult,
troublesome, bothersome, burdensome

tug pull, jerk, wrench, draw, tow, haul, yank

tuition teaching, instruction, education, schooling

tumult noise, uproar, disorder, disturbance, commotion, turmoil, hubbub, racket, fracas, fuss, pandemonium, turbulence, excitement, rumpus, to-do, row *quiet, peace*

tune melody, music, harmony, song

turbulent violent, disorderly, unruly, tumultuous, storming, frenzied, wild, blustering, furious, frantic, excited, riotous *calm, peaceful*

turf grass, sod

turmoil commotion, disturbance, tumult, noise, uproar, disorder, hubbub, racket, fracas, fuss, pandemonium, turbulence, excitement, rumpus, to-do, row *quiet, peace*

turn 1 rotate, pivot, swivel, wheel, twist, gyrate, go around, shift, swerve, veer, curve, circle; 2 change, alter, vary; 3 spoil, sour

tutor teach, instruct, coach, prime, educate, school, enlighten, direct, guide, show, train, drill, prepare, condition

twig branch, limb, sprig, sprout, shoot

twinge pain, pang

twirl spin, rotate, whirl, turn, wind, swivel, wheel, pivot, gyrate

twist 1 turn, wind, curve, rotate, swivel, pivot, wheel, gyrate, circle; 2 change, falsify, misrepresent, distort, disguise, camouflage, alter

type kind, class, group, sort, ilk, variety, species, nature, make, brand, character, genus

typical representative, symbolic, characteristic, distinctive

tyrant dictator, slave driver, despot, oppressor, martinet, taskmaster, disciplinarian

U

ugly 1 unattractive, unsightly, homely, plain, hideous *pretty*; 2 cross, cranky, bad-tempered, disagreeable, unpleasant, quarrelsome, irritable, testy, perverse, mean *pleasant*

ultimate last, final, terminal, conclusive, eventual

umpire judge, referee, moderator, arbitrator, mediator

unable incapable, incompetent, unfit, unqualifiable *able*

unanimous agreed, solid, concurrent, in complete accord

unarmed unprotected, defenceless, unshielded, unequipped *armed*

unassuming modest, meek, humble, unpretentious, natural, genuine, sincere, honest *boastful, arrogant*

unavoidable inevitable, certain, sure, inescapable *uncertain*

unaware ignorant, unknowing, unconscious, unmindful, unsuspecting *aware*

unbearable intolerable, insufferable *tolerable*

unbelievable incredible, doubtful, questionable, unconvincing, suspicious *believable*

unbiased impartial, fair, unprejudiced *prejudiced*

unbroken continuous, uninterrupted, constant, even, regular, steady, perpetual, whole *broken*

uncanny strange, mysterious, weird, creepy, eerie

uncertain doubtful, unsure, speculative, changeable, unpredictable, insecure, precarious *certain, sure*

unchanged same, permanent, unaltered, regular, constant, steady *changed, irregular*

uncivilized barbarous, savage, bestial, wild, brutal, unrefined, uncouth, uncultured *civilized, refined*

uncomfortable distressing, painful, disturbed, bothered, troubled, upset, uneasy *comfortable*

uncommon rare, unusual, unique, novel, different, original, infrequent, scarce *common*

unconcerned uninterested, indifferent, blasé, nonchalant, apathetic, easygoing *concerned, interested*

unconditional unqualified, absolute, unlimited, positive, complete, total, perfect, entire, utter, explicit, express *conditional, limited*

unconscious 1 senseless, out cold; 2 unaware, unintentional, unthinking, preoccupied, absent-minded, oblivious *conscious, aware*

unconstitutional illegal, unlawful, illegitimate, unauthorized *legal*

uncouth awkward, clumsy, crude, ungainly, vulgar, coarse, gross, rude, crass, boorish, unrefined, unpolished, uncultured, uncivilized, barbarous, common, base *genteel, courteous, suave*

uncover reveal, expose, disclose, open, unmask *cover, conceal*

uncultivated wild, undeveloped, rough, crude, fallow *cultivated, refined*

undecided uncertain, unsettled, pending, vague, indefinite, undertermined *certain, settled*

under below, beneath, lower *above*

underfed undernourished, starved

undergo experience, go through, meet, have, feel, encounter, endure, suffer

underhand secret, sly, shifty, surreptitious, deceitful, dishonest, fraudulent, crooked, unscrupulous *open, honest*

undermine weaken, sabotage, destroy

underneath below, beneath, under *above*

underrate minimize, underestimate, belittle *overrate*

understand comprehend, follow, grasp, conceive, realize, know, appreciate

undertake 1 try, attempt, essay, pursue; 2 promise, contract, agree

undesirable objectionable, disagreeable, unpleasant, distasteful, offensive, repulsive, intolerable, loathsome, unsatisfactory, unacceptable, unsuitable *desirable*

undisputed unquestioned, uncontested, accepted, believed, undoubted *questionable*

undisturbed untroubled, calm, tranquil *disturbed*

undo 1 unfasten, untie, disassemble, take apart, dismantle *assemble*; 2 destroy, spoil, abolish, wreck *build*

undress disrobe, unclothe, strip *dress*

unearth dig up, discover, extract, withdraw, remove, uncover, disclose, turn up *bury, hide*

unearthly strange, weird, ghostly, wild, supernatural, odd, queer, peculiar, spooky, uncanny, eerie

uneasy restless, disturbed, anxious, uncomfortable, fidgety, impatient, distressed, troubled, bothered, agitated, perturbed *calm, comfortable*

unemployed idle, jobless, unoccupied, out of work *employed*

unending continuous, endless, uninterrupted, ceaseless, incessant, interminable, perpetual, infinite, everlasting, permanent

unequal uneven, irregular, disparate *equal*

uneven unequal, irregular, disparate *even*

unexpected unforeseen, unanticipated, chance, accidental, sudden *foreseen, expected*

unfair unjust *fair*

unfaithful untrue, disloyal, false, fickle *faithful*

unfamiliar unusual, strange, uncommon, rare, unique, novel, new, different *familiar, common*

unfasten undo, loosen, open, untie, unhook *fasten, close*

unfavourable unsatisfactory, harmful, detrimental, adverse, contrary, uncomplimentary, disapproving *favourable*

unfinished incomplete, rough, undone, crude *finished, completed*

unfit unsuitable, inappropriate, incapable, incompetent, unqualified *fit, suitable*

unfold 1 reveal, show, open, disclose, uncover, unmask, spread, unfurl *hide, conceal*; 2 explain, show, clarify, demonstrate, illuminate

unforeseen unexpected, unanticipated, sudden *expected*

unforgettable memorable, notable, noteworthy, remarkable, extraordinary, exceptional *ordinary*

unfortunate unlucky, ill-fated *lucky, fortunate*

unfriendly unsociable, aloof, standoffish, distant, remote, cool, uncordial, inhospitable *friendly*

ungainly awkward, clumsy, bungling,

unhandy, ungraceful, gawky *graceful*

ungracious impolite, rude, discourteous,
uncivil, ungallant, unkind *gracious, polite*

ungrateful unappreciative, unthankful
grateful, thankful

unhappy sad, sorrowful, uncheerful,
displeased, discontented, wretched,
miserable, dejected, depressed, downcast,
disheartened, despondent, melancholy, blue,
wistful, unsatisfied *happy, cheerful*

unhealthy sickly, infirm, unwholesome,
unsound, weak, feeble, frail, run-down, ill,
ailing, unwell, indisposed *healthy*

uniform 1 even, alike, unvaried, constant,
steady, regular, consistent, symmetrical,
balanced *uneven, irregular*; 2 outfit,
costume

unify combine, unite, consolidate, join, mix,
merge, blend, fuse *separate*

unimportant insignificant, trifling,
inconsequential, trivial, petty *important*

uninhabited unoccupied, deserted, abandoned,
vacant *occupied*

unnecessary needless, uncalled-for,
inessential, superfluous, excess *necessary,
essential*

unnoticed unobserved, unheeded, unseen
noticed, seen

unobserved unnoticed, unheeded, unseen
noticed, seen

unoccupied vacant, idle, deserted, open,
available, uninhabited *occupied*

unpack unload, discharge, dump *pack*

unpaid owing, due, outstanding *paid*

unpleasant disagreeable, distasteful,
unsavoury, undesirable, unlikable, offensive,
odious, repulsive, repugnant, obnoxious
pleasant

unpopular unappreciated, unloved, unwanted, unlikable, unwelcome, disliked *popular, well-liked*

unprecedented unduplicated, uncopied, unimitated, extraordinary, exceptional

unprepared unready, unwary *ready*

unprofitable unrewarding, fruitless *profitable, rewarding*

unquestionable certain, positive, undeniable, indisputable *questionable, dubious*

unravel 1 unsnarl, untwist, disentangle *tangle*; 2 solve, explain, answer, resolve, figure out, unriddle, decipher, decode, crack

unreal 1 imaginary, fanciful, fictitious; 2 counterfeit, make-believe, false, mock, imitation, simulated, ungenuine, unauthentic, artificial, synthetic, pseudo, fake *real*

unreasonable extreme, excessive, outrageous, preposterous, extravagant, impractical, illogical, senseless, inconsistent, irrational, unsound *reasonable, moderate*

unrest restlessness, agitation, disquiet, stir, disturbance, commotion, turmoil, tumult, excitement *calm, peacefulness*

unrivalled unmatched, unequalled, incomparable

unruly disorderly, riotous, wild, rampant, lawless *orderly*

unsafe dangerous, unsound, precarious, imperilled, risky, perilous, hazardous *safe*

unsatisfactory ungratifying, inadequate insufficient, inferior, second-rate, low-grade *satisfactory*

unscrupulous dishonest, unprincipled, unethical, corrupt, crooked, criminal, fraudulent *honest, moral*

unselfish generous, liberal, free, unsparing, lavish, open-handed, bighearted, magnanimous *selfish*

unsettle disturb, shake, upset, startle, shock

unshaken firm, resolute, staunch, solid, fixed, unyielding, steady *shaken*

unsightly ugly, unattractive, homely, plain *pretty, attractive*

unskilled untrained, untalented, inexperienced, raw, green, amateurish *skilled, talented*

unsophisticated simple, natural, artless, naive, green *sophisticated*

unstable unsteady, weak, unsound, unreliable, unsure, unsafe *stable, reliable*

unsteady unstable, weak, unsound, unreliable, unsure, unsafe *steady, reliable*

unsuccessful failing, unfortunate, abortive, fruitless *successful*

unsuitable unfit, inappropriate, unbecoming, improper, unsatisfactory, objectionable, unacceptable *suitable, proper*

unthinkable unbelievable, incredible, impossible, inconceivable, absurd, ridiculous, preposterous, outlandish, unheard-of *believable*

untidy neglected, slovenly, shabby, frowzy, messy, sloppy, seedy *tidy, neat*

untie loosen, unfasten, undo *tie*

untrained unskilled, unprepared, untalented, inexperienced, amateurish, raw, green *trained, skilled*

untried new, unused, untouched, unproved *tried, tested*

untrue 1 false, wrong, faulty, erroneous, fallacious *true, right*; 2 unfaithful, disloyal, fickle *faithful, loyal*

unused 1 new, fresh, firsthand, original,
untouched *used*; 2 unaccustomed,
unfamiliar with *used to*

unusual uncommon, rare, unique, out of the
ordinary, novel, queer, odd, different *usual,
ordinary*

unwelcome unwanted, uninvited *welcome*

unwell ailing, ill, sick, indisposed *well,
healthy*

unwieldy unmanageable, unhandy, awkward,
clumsy, cumbersome, bulky *manageable*

unwilling reluctant, forced, involuntary,
disinclined *willing*

unwise foolish, unreasonable, unsound,
senseless, irrational *wise*

unyielding firm, stubborn, immovable,
inflexible, unpliable, unbending, adamant,
rigid *flexible*

uphold support, confirm, sustain, maintain,
bolster, substantiate, corroborate

upkeep maintenance, support, backing,
provision

upper higher, superior, greater *lower*

upright 1 standing, erect, vertical *prone*;
2 honourable, upstanding, reputable,
respectable, moral, law-abiding

uprising revolt, rebellion, mutiny,
insurrection, riot, revolution

uproar noise, disturbance, commotion, hubbub,
tumult, clamour, turmoil, racket, fracas, ado,
fuss, pandemonium, rumpus, to-do, row
peace, quiet

uproot extract, withdraw, remove, pull out

upset 1 overturn, tip over, unsettle, capsize;
2 disturb, perturb, trouble, agitate, confuse,
shake, fluster, ruffle, bother, unnerve *soothe,
calm*; 3 overthrow, defeat, revolution,
overwhelm

up-to-date modern, contemporary, advanced, current, fashionable *old-fashioned, outdated*

urban metropolitan, civic, municipal, citified *suburban*

urge push, force, drive, plead, advise, incite, press, pressure, coax, goad, prod, spur, agitate, provoke, prompt *discourage*

urgent pressing, important, imperative, compelling, crucial, essential, vital, necessary, moving, motivating, driving *unimportant*

usage method, practice, way, use, procedure, treatment, handling

use 1 utilize, employ, practise, exercise, handle, manage; 2 exploit, take advantage of

useful helpful, beneficial, profitable, serviceable, advantageous, practical, functional, handy, valuable *useless*

useless worthless, ineffectual, fruitless *useful*

usual customary, ordinary, normal, regular, common, everyday, typical *unusual*

usurp take command, take charge, take over, assume control, overthrow, seize command

utilize use, employ

utmost greatest, farthest, highest, extreme, most

V

vacant unoccupied, empty, void, barren, desolate *occupied, filled*

vaccinate inoculate, immunize

vague unclear, indistinct, indefinite, dim, faint, shadowy, obscure, blurred, fuzzy, hazy, misty *clear, definite*

vain 1 unsuccessful, ineffectual, futile, fruitless *successful*; 2 proud, conceited, boastful, egotistical, egocentric, haughty, lofty, self-centred *humble*

valiant   brave, courageous, bold, gallant, heroic, chivalrous, daring, unafraid, dauntless   *cowardly*

valid   sound, true, good, effective, proven, established, well-grounded, cogent, legal, lawful, adequate, authorized   *invalid, false*

value   worth, excellence, usefulness, importance, significance, weight, merit, quality

vandal   destroyer, wrecker, demolisher

vanish   disappear, fade, go away, perish, cease to be   *appear*

vanquish   conquer, defeat, overcome, subdue, crush

various   different, several, many, diverse

varnish   1 paint, coat, lacquer, shellac; 2 distort, falsify, misrepresent, colour, disguise, camouflage

vary   change, differ, alter, deviate

vast   large, immense, great, enormous, huge, stupendous, colossal, monumental, mammoth, gigantic   *tiny*

vault   1 jump, leap, spring, hop, bound, hurdle; 2 storehouse, compartment, depository, safe, coffer;   3 burial place, crypt, tomb

vegetation   plants, flora, growth

veil   cover, screen, hide, conceal, cloak, mask, disguise, camouflage, eclipse, obscure   *unveil, uncover*

velocity   speed, swiftness, quickness

vengeance   revenge, retaliation, reprisal, avengement

ventilate   1 air, aerate, refresh, cool; 2 discuss, reason, talk over, deliberate, consider, treat, examine, study

venture   undertaking, enterprise, project, attempt, adventure, experiment

verbal oral, spoken, uttered, said, vocalized, voiced, pronounced, sounded, articulated, enunciated *written*

verdict decision, judgment, finding, determination, decree, ruling, pronouncement

verge 1 tend, incline, lean, border; 2 edge, rim, brink, border

verify confirm, prove, certify, validate, substantiate, authenticate, corroborate, support, document, double-check

versatile skilled, talented, competent, capable, many-sided, adaptable, all-round

verse 1 poetry, rhyme, jingle; 2 section, chapter, passage, part, division, measure

version rendition, account, interpretation

vertical standing, upright, perpendicular, erect

very greatly, extremely, much, exceedingly, quite, pretty, intensely

vessel 1 container, receptacle; 2 ship, boat

veteran 1 experienced, practised, worldly-wise, sophisticated; 2 ex-soldier

veto refuse, deny *accept*

vibrate shake, quiver, quake, tremble, quaver, wobble, bob, bounce

vice fault, bad habit, weakness, failing, foible, shortcoming, wrongdoing, malpractice, sin, crime

vicinity 1 region, area, zone, territory, place, district, quarter, section, neighbourhood; 2 nearness, closeness, proximity

vicious evil, wicked, spiteful, malicious, bad, naughty, wrong, sinful, base, low, vile, cruel, ruthless, brutal, barbarous, savage, ferocious, inhumane *kind, good*

victim prey, dupe, loser, underdog, sufferer

victory success, triumph, conquest, winning, win, knockout *defeat*

view　1 see, sight, look at, behold, observe, perceive, watch, regard;　2 opinion, belief, attitude, sentiment, feeling, impression, notion, idea, thought, conception, theory, judgment, outlook

vigorous　strong, energetic, potent, powerful, mighty, forceful, rugged, hearty, robust, dynamic, intense, active, lively, animated, spirited, vivacious　*weak*

vile　foul, disgusting, bad, terrible, dreadful, horrible, deplorable, outrageous, wretched, base, odious, obnoxious, abominable, detestable, despicable, contemptible

vindicate　justify, uphold, defend successfully, pardon, excuse, forgive, acquit

vindictive　revengeful, avenging

violate　break, trespass, infringe

violence　anger, rage, passion, fury, force, intensity, vehemence

virgin　pure, spotless, unused, new, firsthand, original, fresh, green　*used, old*

virtuous　good, moral, righteous, angelic, saintly, chaste, pure, innocent, faultless, sinless　*sinful, wicked*

visible　apparent, manifest, noticeable, open, exposed, perceptible, evident, obvious, plain, clear　*concealed*

vision　1 sight, perception;　2 apparition, image, illusion, phantom, fantasy, dream, spectre, ghost

visit　attend, go to, call on, drop in

vital　1 necessary, important, essential, fundamental, needed, required *unimportant*;　2 living, alive, animate

vitality　strength, vigour, might, potency, power, energy, stamina

vivid　bright, brilliant, strong, clear, distinct, splendid, flamboyant, glaring, dazzling, rich, colourful　*dull*

vocal spoken, uttered, said, voiced, pronounced, sounded, oral, verbal, articulated, enunciated

vocation occupation, business, profession, trade, work, line, calling, craft

vogue fashion, style, mode, popularity

voice express, utter, verbalize, say, articulate, enunciate, pronounce, communicate, tell

void 1 empty, vacant, bare, blank, barren, desolate, unoccupied, deserted, open, available *filled*; 2 invalid *valid*

volume 1 amount, quantity, capacity, content, proportion, measure, extent; 2 book, publication, writing, work

volunteer offer, come forward

vomit retch, heave, regurgitate, spew, throw up

vote ballot, choice, voice, poll, referendum, designation, selection, decision, determination

vow swear, promise, assure, guarantee, vouch, pledge

voyage journey, travel, sail, cruise, navigate

vulgar coarse, common, unrefined, indecent, improper, offensive, crude, crass, obscene, uncouth, foul, filthy, nasty *refined*

vulnerable sensitive, exposed, open, susceptible, unprotected, defenseless

W

wage 1 pay, payment, salary, remuneration, compensation,; 2 pursue, conduct, carry on, practise, exercise, follow, engage in

wager bet, gamble, hazard, stake

wail cry, screech, shriek, scream, squeal, howl, bawl, moan

wait delay, postpone, defer, put off, shelve, table, procrastinate, stay, tarry, linger

wake awake, arise, get up, rouse, arouse, stir

walk step, tread, pace, ambulate, stroll, hike

wander stray, meander, roam, rove, gad, drift, ramble

wane decrease, diminish, lessen, decline, subside, recede *increase, wax*

want 1 desire, wish for, like, long for, fancy; 2 need, lack, require

war fight, conflict, strife, battle, combat, engagement, encounter, clash, struggle, hostilities, campaign

warehouse storehouse, depository, depot

warm 1 hot, tepid; 2 friendly, enthusiastic, cordial, congenial *cold*

warn 1 inform, give notice, notify, caution, forebode, advise, alert; 2 threaten, menace

warrant 1 authority, right, sanction, authorization, certificate, justification, reason, voucher, writ, mandate; 2 guarantee, pledge, promise, vow, word, assurance, oath

warrior soldier, fighter

wary cautious, careful, guarded, suspicious, distrustful

wash clean, scrub, launder, bathe, rinse, scour

waste 1 spend, squander, consume, use up, exhaust *save*; 2 garbage, refuse, scraps, dregs, rubbish

watch 1 look at, view, observe, regard; 2 guard, protect, mind, tend, shield, care for

waterway channel, river, canal, passageway

wave 1 sway, move, flap, flutter, swing; 2 signal, gesture

wax 1 increase, gain, grow, rise, swell, heighten, intensify, enlarge, develop, sprout, flourish *decrease, wane*; 2 polish, burnish, furbish, glaze, shine

way 1 manner, style, custom, mode, fashion, usage, practice; 2 means, method, procedure, process; 3 point, feature, detail, respect; 4 direction, line, course; 5 distance, reach, remoteness, length, extent; 6 will, nature, character, constitution, temperament, disposition, mood, humour

weak feeble, powerless, impotent, debilitated, fragile *strong, sturdy*

wealth riches, affluence, prosperity, abundance, opulence, possessions, fortune, treasure, resources, assets *poverty*

wear 1 dress in, have on, don; 2 deteriorate, corrode, decay *worn*

weary tired, fatigued, weak, faint, listless, lethargic, sluggish *lively, energetic*

weather climate, the elements

wedge jam, push, lodge, squeeze

weep cry, shed tears, sob, bawl, blubber, snivel

weigh measure, gauge, assess, estimate, rate, appraise, size up

weighty 1 heavy, hefty *light*; 2 burdensome, oppressive, onerous; 3 important, influential, powerful, effective, serious *trivial*

weird strange, mysterious, odd, fantastic, queer, creepy, peculiar, spooky, eerie, ghostly *normal*

welcome greet, receive

welfare well-being, good, benefit, interest, advantage, behalf, prosperity, success, comfort

whether if, provided, on condition

whiff odour, smell, scent, fume

whim fancy, notion, caprice, fad, phase

whimper cry, whine

whip strike, beat, thrash, spank, flog, pummel, lash, lace, strap, paddle

whirl spin, turn, wheel, twirl, reel, swirl, rotate, pivot, swivel, gyrate

whisper murmur, mutter, mumble

whole complete, total, entire, one, solid, undivided *partial*

wholehearted earnest, sincere, hearty, cordial, gracious *insincere*

wholesome healthful, beneficial, salutary, sound

wicked 1 bad, evil, sinful, vicious, naughty, wrong, base, low, vile *good, saintly*; 2 difficult, rough, hard, unpleasant, severe, rugged, tough *easy, pleasant*

wide broad, extensive, expansive, roomy, ample, spacious, far-reaching *narrow*

wield hold, wave, handle, manipulate, use, employ, manage, control

wig hairpiece, toupee

wiggle wriggle, squirm, writhe, twist, fidget, jerk, twitch, toss

wild 1 untamed, uncivilized, savage, unchecked, unrestrained, violent, barbarous, brutal, rampant, fierce, ferocious, bestial *tame*; 2 rash, crazy, reckless, impetuous, furious, mad, wanton, frantic, frenzied, rabid, delirious, hysterical, overwrought *calm*

wilderness wasteland

will 1 wish, desire, pleasure, fancy, hope, urge, inclination, volition; 2 resolution, determination, decision, resolve, purpose, choice, selection, election, intention, design, plan, contemplation; 3 bequest, legacy, testament

willing ready, consenting, agreeable, inclined, compliant, eager *unwilling*

wilt wither, deteriorate, pine, droop, fade, shrivel, dry up, languish *flourish*

wily tricky, cunning, crafty, sly, artful, shifty, smooth, slippery, foxy, canny, shrewd, clever

win gain, capture, carry, succeed, triumph, be victorious, prevail *lose*

1. wind 1 air, draft, breeze, gust; 2 breathe, respiration

2. wind turn, bend, twist, roll, coil, spiral, pivot, swivel

winning charming, attractive, alluring, fascinating, captivating, lovely, enchanting, enthralling, intriguing, bewitching, interesting, delightful, appealing, enticing, inviting, tantalizing, provocative, fetching *repulsive*

wiry 1 lean, stringy *stout*; 2 strong, tough, muscular, athletic, brawny *weak*

wise bright, smart, knowledgeable, sage, knowing, learned, profound, educated, cultured, scholarly *dull, uneducated*

wish want, desire, long for, like, fancy, request

wistful longing, yearning, desirous, pining, hankering, nostalgic, homesick, melancholy, pensive

wit humour, intelligence, understanding, sense

witch hag, vixen, shrew, sorceress

withdraw 1 retreat, recede, retire, fall back, reverse, quit, vacate, abandon *advance*; 2 remove, subtract, deduct, extract *deposit*

wither fade, shrivel, dry up, shrink, wane, deteriorate, droop, wilt, languish, pine *flourish*

withhold 1 reserve, keep, save, preserve *spend*; 2 refuse, deny, disallow *give*

within inside, in *outside*

without lacking, wanting, needing, missing, short of, minus, less *with*

withstand endure, resist, oppose, repel
succumb, give in

witness 1 testify, vouch, swear; 2 see, observe,
behold, view, perceive, discern, glimpse, spy,
sight

witty clever, amusing, humorous, funny,
whimsical, droll *dull*

wizard 1 sorcerer, conjuror; 2 expert, master,
genius

wobbly unsteady, shaky, wavering, rickety,
trembling *steady*

woe grief, trouble, distress, misery, anguish,
agony, heartache, desolation, oppression,
sorrow *happiness*

wonder 1 marvel, gape, stare; 2 doubt,
question, be uncertain, not know

wonderful marvellous, remarkable, striking,
astonishing, incredible, extraordinary,
exceptional, superb, magnificent, miraculous,
splendid, fabulous *ordinary, plain*

word phrase, say, express, put, voice, tell,
communicate

work 1 labour, toil, accomplish, achieve, effect,
make, busy, occupy, engage, employ;
2 operate, run, manage, conduct, handle,
manipulate, manoeuvre

workout 1 exercise, practice, drill; 2 trial,
test, rehearsal, dry run, tryout

world universe, earth, globe

worn 1 damaged, old, secondhand, used,
impaired, ragged *new*; 2 tired, wearied,
fatigued, weak, faint *energetic*

worry bother, trouble, torment, molest, harass,
harry, badger, plague, vex *soothe, console*

worse deteriorated, impaired, aggravated

worship respect, honour, idolize, adore, revere,
admire, cherish

worth   merit, usefulness, importance, value, benefit, significance, weight

wound   1 harm, hurt, injure, damage, bruise *heal*;   2 irritate, provoke, sting, infuriate, madden, pain, grieve, offend *soothe*

wrap   cover, envelop, sheathe, surround, encompass, bind *uncover*

wreck   destroy, ruin, devastate, ravage, demolish, dismantle, disassemble

wrench   1 pull, twist, jerk, tear from, wrest, yank;   2 sprain, injure, hurt, strain

wrestle   struggle, battle, fight, tussle

wretch   1 beggar, sufferer, poor devil, derelict;   2 scoundrel, villain, knave, rogue, shrew

wriggle   twist, turn, wiggle, squirm, writhe

wring   twist, squeeze, press out, wrest

writ   notice, order, warrant

write   record, inscribe, mark, note, post, pen, scribe

wrong   1 incorrect, improper, unfit, unsuitable, untrue, false, mistaken *right*;   2 bad, evil, ill *good*

X

Y

yard   1 court, pen, enclosure, confine;   2 three feet

yell   shout, cry out, call, howl, scream, shriek, whoop, roar, bellow, wail, squall, bawl

yield   1 produce, give, grant, bear, provide, supply, furnish;   2 surrender, give up, relinquish, waive, forego, part with, sacrifice *keep, retain*

young   youthful, juvenile *old*

youngster   child, minor, youth

Z

zeal enthusiasm, eagerness, sincerity, ardour, fervour, passion *indifference, apathy*

zero nothing, naught, nil, none

zest relish, enjoyment, gusto, savour, delight, eagerness, pleasure, satisfaction

zone region, area, territory, place, district, quarter, section, division, part, department, compartment, vicinity, neighbourhood

zoo menagerie, animal enclosure